WORTHY
AND PREPARED

A simple guide to the two essential principles

to help your organization raise more money

and to help the causes that are important to us all

ED SLUGA, CFRE
& PETER BARROW

civil sector press

WORTHY AND PREPARED
A SIMPLE GUIDE TO THE TWO ESSENTIAL PRINCIPLES TO HELP
YOUR ORGANIZATION RAISE MORE MONEY AND TO HELP THE
CAUSES THAT ARE IMPORTANT TO US ALL

ISBN# 1-895589-64-9

Published by Civil Sector Press
Box 86, Station C,
Toronto, Ontario, M6J 3M7 Canada
Telephone: 416-345-9403
Fax: 416-345-8010

Printed in Canada by: Harmony Printing
Design by: Creative by Nature

Authors' note concerning the use of examples in Worthy and Prepared:

All the examples used in Worthy and Prepared are drawn from real life
situations either known to the authors or in the public domain. Some
names and facts may have been changed to protect the privacy and
confidentiality of the organizations involved. But the lessons learned are
real!

DEDICATION

PETER'S DEDICATION

To the many volunteers and donors who are a huge part of the success story of the Children's Foundation of Guelph and Wellington, with thanks for letting me be a part of it all. And to Fiona, Chris, Cam, Caleb and Chloe, who are my world.

ED'S DEDICATION

Thanks to all the great people who work tirelessly for charities and not-for-profits for low pay and little recognition. You truly are making the world a better place. And to Claire, Jack and Jodie for making my world a better place.

TABLE OF CONTENTS

FOREWORD

Amid reduced government funding, diminishing returns on some traditional programs and increased public and media pressure for cost effectiveness, board and organizational leaders are increasingly attracted to the world of major gift fundraising. In so doing they can be very successful, but in too many cases they inadvertently expose their worthy organizations to tremendous risk. Poor major gift fundraising can have catastrophic impacts on an organization, its reputation and perhaps most paradoxically, its viability. That is why I am honoured to be able to introduce you to *Worthy and Prepared*, an important and accessible work for those in or concerned about the non-profit fundraising sector.

Using accounts that are closer to fact than fiction, Ed Sluga and Peter Barrow describe grass roots organizations facing the same fundraising challenges many of us face everyday. These organizations are often led by passionate volunteers and staff champions who are well-intentioned and self-less. Unfortunately this same passion can result in emotion replacing reason and hope replacing sound strategy.

A friend once told me that the challenge with being a school teacher is that anyone who attended school thinks they know how to teach. As a veteran fundraiser, I have often found myself thinking about that analogy as I sat with people who, because they had sold chocolate almonds or participated in a United Way workplace giving campaign, honestly considered themselves to be a fundraiser. Sometimes when strategy needs to be developed and ambitious revenue targets met, fact-based and honest assessments of capacity can be replaced by bold, aggressive and not viable strategies. While understandable, this oversimplification can be quite dangerous.

The challenge of course is that what appears to be simple is far from it. I have good news. You are reading a play book with specific steps and a process to enable you to spot the pitfalls and develop the due diligence required in order to become a successful fundraising organization. *Worthy and Prepared* contains tools to enable you to honestly assess your state of fundraising sophistication and preparedness and some fairly dire warning of the consequences of not doing so. Unfortunately, there are no shortcuts. This is perhaps the key learning of the entire work.

Rather than provide examples of mega-organization successes that are not relevant to most of us, Ed and Peter focus on examples of organizations that lead their sectors using sound management, inspired leadership and a clear and loudly articulated vision.

Although it contains best practices targeted towards smaller shops, it is in fact a reference that should be required reading for every non-profit executive – fundraiser or otherwise.

Quite a bit of attention is paid to explaining the process of brand development and management and reputation protection. Senior staff and volunteers must be vocal and passionate champions of your organization and your community must be aware of what you do and the difference that you make. You need to tell your story effectively and ensure that instead of communicating with donors you are connecting with them. This is delicate work, and while it is tempting to produce marketing materials internally to avoid spending donor dollars, this is a false economy. Donors expect you to be present and professional in the marketplace and you will do much to earn and continue to enjoy their support if you build a stature and reputation that provides proof of ROI to your supporters. Donors are like investors and they want proof of concept and assurance that your organization is vested and is viable and has the capacity and the discipline to do the work that needs to be done. This sounds like a lot of work and it is, but the result is stakeholders – volunteers, staff and donors – who deeply believe that the organization is worthy of a large gift.

Another false economy is to avoid using consultants. The chapter on how to retain and manage consultants and what you can expect them to do – and not do – is critical and balanced.

Our authors both walk the walk and talk the talk. Ed Sluga and Peter Barrow are active volunteer leaders in their communities. They combine fundraising wisdom with real life corporate experience. *Worthy and Prepared* is a wise and practical and affirming work – I would have made fewer mistakes had I read it 20 years ago. It has gentleness and wisdom and is as much a self-help book and management book as a fundraising book.

I strongly recommend this book. Enjoy.

KEN MAYHEW

CHIEF FUNDRAISING OFFICER

MS SOCIETY OF CANADA

ACKNOWLEDGEMENTS

Thanks to all those organizations and people that have made this book possible. Through working with many organizations, we have had our successes – and failures – and we have met many individuals who have taught us a great deal about passion for a cause, working hard toward a goal and letting people express their true beliefs through their actions and their generosity.

These people include:

Suzanne Bone, Executive Director of The Foundation of Guelph General Hospital

The Board and staff of the Children's Foundation of Guelph and Wellington

Nancy Collett, Senior Development Officer of the University of Toronto Faculty of Medicine

Sue Egles, Partner of Inspire Fundraising Consulting

Ken Mayhew, Chief Fundraising Officer, MS Society of Canada

Curt Hammond, President, Pearl Street

Jim Hilborn, The Hilborn Group

Leanne Hitchcock, Publisher and everyone at Civil Sector Press

Cecil Barron Jensen, Executive Director of the Artists Association of Nantucket

Doug MacMillan, CEO, MacMillan Marketing Inc

Jone Mitchell, Vice President of Advancement of Mount St. Vincent University

George Stanois of The Goldie Company

And thanks to the late Dr. Edward Pearce of Queen's University, whose character, wisdom and intelligence were some of the main inspirations for this book.

INTRODUCTION
WORTHY AND PREPARED: SELF-HELP
FOR THE CHARITABLE ORGANIZATION

Some years ago during a break at a board retreat session for a small charity, a Director mentioned reading about a major charitable gift that had just been announced in a prominent national newspaper.

The Director's small charity was based in an agricultural area an hour's drive from a major metropolitan centre. Over time, the area had slowly become filled with the extremely wealthy who were converting old farms into country residences. Equestrian centres and high-end private golf facilities were very much part of the scene.

The Director had recently become neighbour to an extremely wealthy and internationally known businessman. The newspaper announcement focused on a multi-million dollar gift from this neighbour to a charity. Not, alas, to the charity supported by the Director, but instead to a large research hospital attached to a high-profile university in the nearby large city.

"Why?" asked the Director, "would he give a gift to them and not to us? He lives right beside me in this community. Why didn't we get his gift?"

The answer was simple enough. The donor found that the charity of his choice matched his own values and expectations. In short, he found it to be Worthy and Prepared.

Conversely, the donor didn't consider the Director's charity – if he knew about it at all – as being worthy of support – neighbourliness notwithstanding.

It's easy to understand the Director's question that day. It is equally easy to find fault with his simple argument. The position you take may indicate which side of the worthy and prepared equation you support.

One side says that donors give to people they know and like and that this is often all you need to attract funding.

The other side says that, even though relationships between donors and recipients are vital, what is much more important is that the

ORGANIZATION, as a whole, is worthy of support and prepared enough to receive it.

We are firmly on the side of those who say that being worthy of a donor's support and being prepared to turn that support into action are the essentials to securing major gifts.

Whether the organization is worthy by default, by association or by design, that worthiness is the first key to securing a transformational gift. Being prepared for the new relationship is also extremely important. Can the organization's practices cope with a larger gift and all the expectations that it brings? Does the organization instill confidence in the donor by what it does and how it operates? How is that confidence instilled? How is that reinforced on a daily basis? In discussions with many fundraising professionals from all types of organizations, as well as other areas of professional practice, the core message of "You need to be Worthy and Prepared" is greeted time and again with the sort of immediate recognition that many such self-help messages often receive.

The message itself is simple. Putting it into practice is more difficult. We all want to believe that we are ready for big gifts and significant donations. We all want to try and make it happen. But time and again, at every level of the charitable world, evidence abounds that most organizations, even those successful in gathering community support, are not, in fact, advancing the basics of being Worthy and Prepared.

As a result, they are not raising the funds they could be raising, not focusing on the best possible ways to raise money and not focusing on what this book calls "their destiny proposition." Creating a climate of giving through worthiness and preparation is hard work. There is no easy way around it.

One important challenge is that it is difficult to pin down exactly what being Worthy and Prepared means. In some ways it is a state of mind – a philosophical acceptance that certain standards need to be met for maximum success by even the smallest of charities.

But that state of mind must be accepted by all three segments of an organization that are charged with creating and benefiting from the concept: the Board, staff and volunteers. This book explains how that can be achieved, so that small charities in particular can be successful in raising funds, most notably larger gifts.

It also provides many practical and pragmatic things to consider, steps to take and fundamental ways to operate that are at the core of every truly Worthy and Prepared organization. This is more than a fundraising book. It is more than a management book. This is a self-help book for your organization. As an organization, what makes you "worthy"? And, once that is established, how do you become truly "prepared"?

To be successful, the organization must constantly think like a leader. It must set the highest standards, expect the most from all its important internal stakeholders, take bold steps, possess the courage to try new things and the confidence that it can fail and still succeed.

In short, it has to be Worthy and Prepared.

WORTHY AND PREPARED:
WELL INTENTIONED... BUT

For the seven volunteer board members of the Good Food Group (GFG), gathered together on their own time this Saturday morning, the fundraising planning session that they had so eagerly anticipated was not going well.

It had started with great expectations.

"We're here to see if we can double our current operating revenues in two years," said the hired gun facilitator with all the optimism and gusto of his calling.

"We need to take a look at everything we are doing now and ask, "How can we do it better, more creatively, more profitably and, of utmost importance, in ways that benefit the organization and its members?"

Everyone nodded enthusiastically. This was certainly why they were there. The organization badly needed new revenues to help it offer its parcels of food and other necessities for elderly people still living on the streets.

It needed funds to recruit new members, to market itself effectively, to train more counselors, to create new ways to provide physical, emotional, financial and spiritual help for those most in need – and, above all, to increase its ability to generate donations of food and distribute them effectively.

In short, it needed far more financial stability in a hurry. It had to find ways to do this at a time when the economy was making fundraising even tougher than usual and making it harder for volunteers to break away from their own pressures and time constraints to support the agency.

For the first few hours, the group worked energetically in one of the peaceful salons of a local funeral home, generously donated for the day by one of its members.

It conducted its own SWOT analysis (Strengths, Weaknesses, Opportunities and Threats), set goals for the future and analyzed the gap between where it was now financially and where it needed to be. It even came up with several action plans ("building blocks," the facilitator termed them with typical consultant-speak) to get them from A to B.

Then came the moment of truth, the time when, as the facilitator said, "The rubber meets the road." The group had to develop costs for the action plans and set a fundraising goal for the future.

As the late afternoon sun bathed the room in a golden glow, three things happened to the volunteers.

First, they realized that their educated guesses about what things cost, were just that – guesses. They would need to do far more work to determine real costs: work that could only be done by their already over-burdened staff or by them. None of them really had the time or knowledge to do what was required. Nor, truth be told, did they have the inclination on top of all their other volunteer commitments.

There was a real danger that they would fall victim to "analysis-paralysis," unable to move forward because of lack of time and resources.

Second, the group recognized that doubling current revenues over two years sounded good on paper. In reality, however, this meant a 100% increase (in their case a total of $250,000) – a daunting figure that, beyond great ideas, they did not know how to achieve. How could they ever raise such a huge amount in an increasingly tough economic environment?

Third, and most critically, the one person who might be able to steer them through this – the Executive Director – confronted them with a painful truth.

"You hired me as an administrator, not a fundraiser," she said. "I'd be lying if I told you I know how to raise this money. In fact, I'm scared of doing it. I'd probably rather quit than take it on."

Suddenly, all the energy that had filled the room evaporated like mist in the morning. It seemed as if all the great work of the day had gone for naught. Confronted with the reality of their situation, the volunteers found themselves fearful and frustrated, unable to move forward effectively, to see what had to be done next.

In that moment, they recognized what so many charities today are discovering. No matter how noble their cause or how dedicated they were, no matter how many people depended on them, if they wanted to be successful in fundraising, they had to learn to be Truly Ready.

In other words, they had to become Worthy. And they had to be Prepared.

PART I

CHAPTER 1:
WHAT THE WORD WORTHY REALLY MEANS

There are hundreds of thousands of registered charities in North America. Foundations, Hospitals, Art Galleries, Churches, Schools, Libraries, Sports Teams, Humane Societies, Children's Camps, Service Clubs – the list goes on and on.

The largest charities raise millions – sometimes hundreds of millions – of dollars annually. The smallest may raise only a few thousand dollars every year.

But, large or small, they all compete for the same finite resources – the generosity of those who give to charities and the funds that these good people donate.

Almost all of them are good causes. Who can argue with a society to care for donkeys, charities that send needy kids to camp, ones that strive to find a cure for cancer or diabetes, to help build a House of God or to aid those who have lost children far too early in life?

Similarly, few will take issue with the need to preserve art and culture, to eradicate AIDS and poverty in the Third World, to provide support services for the disabled or food banks for the poor.

On the surface, it would seem that every organization with a big heart and a good cause deserves support from the public that they serve. It should be easy to raise the money it needs to do its best work and to survive, grow and prosper.

But – and it's a huge but – this is not the case. Of those hundreds of thousands of charities, only a few raise truly significant dollars to support their mission. The rest of them struggle to make ends meet or rely on the patronage of just a few supporters to get by. This is not a recipe for long-term success. Nor is it a formula for the organization to accomplish what it has set out to do.

To misuse a well-known phrase: When it comes to raising money successfully, many charities will come calling – but few are chosen!

What separates the "haves" from the "have nots" – especially those charities with budgets of less than $2 million in funds annually – is that the "haves" instinctively understand a vital equation:

Destiny + Process = Success

Those who figure out what this means and strive to make it happen, almost invariably succeed and become financially self-sustaining. They become truly Worthy and they learn to be Prepared.

But before we focus on the Destiny equation, let's pause to look at what being "Worthy" really means. The term seems a little dated in today's fast-paced world where every day brings a new buzzword.

"Worthy" suggests a maiden aunt full of virtue or Lady Bracknell in Oscar Wilde's famous play *The Importance of Being Earnest*. It conjures up pictures of lace tablecloths and dusty teapots, of oil lamps and antimacassars of the long-past Victorian or Edwardian eras.

In short, it doesn't resonate. But it should.

Simply put, being worthy in the context of getting money from other people to support your cause means **Making the Giving Connection.**

It means creating that instant when the cause of the organization connects strongly on an emotional and, sometimes spiritual level with donors and volunteers, so that they give generously of their time and money.

The key words here are "connect" and "emotional." Until you truly reach out and touch the hearts and minds of those you want to help you, you will never be worthy in the true sense of fundraising.

Yes, your cause may be outstanding. It may fill a true need. It may help thousands and thousands of people. It may create new jobs and infrastructure and fill a place in your community that no other organization can fill. It is a noble cause, a just one, a REAL one.

But it only becomes "worthy" in the fundraising sense of the word when it fundamentally connects with the hearts and minds of givers so that they passionately and truly believe in what it does. They experience emotions about it that transcend any regular interactions they may have with other organizations.

As we will see later in this book, there are many ways to become worthy.

You can achieve worthiness when donors and volunteers have a direct personal interest in what you do and why you do it. They support your cause because it closely mirrors what they believe. Those who have lost children may connect to associations that support bereaved families. Those who love animals may connect to the local Humane Society. Those who have experienced the horrors of drunk driving may feel touched by Mothers Against Drunk Driving; while those who believe passionately in the way society should work may reach out to political parties to give them an emotional connection to the governing process.

You may become worthy by association: the role you play in a community, the strength of your brand image, the calibre of the people who sit on your Board and the way in which you tell your story may encourage donors to be attracted to your obvious success and connect with you by giving you funds.

Many hospitals have discovered this to be true. They provide a vital service that ultimately, everyone needs. They have strong and well-respected Board members. They work hard to build their brand and they generally spend a significant amount of money to tell their story. By association, you want to be a part of that, to give something back to an organization that clearly gives so much to others and attracts such powerful people to its cause.

You can also achieve worthiness by working hard and actually creating a need for people to support you that did not seem to exist before. This is a little like McDonalds; it identified the need for fast food and then filled it brilliantly. In marketing terms, it **changed the conversation** about how fast food was ordered and eaten – and the rest is history.

As an example, small, local sports associations can best raise money and connect if they change the conversation for support. Giving money is not about buying equipment, court time or bus fare so that little Jodie and Jack can play basketball. These are the basic needs and not terribly sexy – certainly not of great interest to potential donors. What's more boring than buying court time?

But when you change the conversation, it's about the physical, emotional and character development that participation in sports creates. It's about learning new skills, making new friends and developing a moral understanding of the value of winning and losing. Changing the conversation in that way is hard work, but it can pay off in spades if you do it right. And you can still use the money to buy court time!

Some organizations are worthy in global terms, with a cause that transcends national and international boundaries and develops strength and momentum that sweeps millions of donors up in the passion that it generates. Doctors Without Borders is such an organization. So are Greenpeace, the World Wildlife Fund, The International Red Cross, Save The Children or the Terry Fox Foundation.

You can become worthy by filling a very specific niche that may appeal to a relatively limited number of people. The John Howard Society relates most specifically to those who have been touched by prison in some way. Princess Margaret Hospital in Toronto reaches out just to those with cancer. Universities reach out to their alumni in the hope that they recall great days in the hallowed halls and wish to share the experience with others.

Still others relate specifically to a community. Your local Hospice is an example, as is any parish church or local service club. Any community event that has a reputation of its own and needs to sustain itself is often worthy of support. The local arts festival, the highland games, the annual concert or even a pig roast: all merit support if they connect emotionally at some level with donors.

Finally, you may become worthy through your connection to a specific circumstance. Natural disasters, human tragedies, sudden medical emergencies, economic chaos or political instability all create their own set of emotional connections that prompt others to give support and to keep on giving it long after the actual event has passed. Food Banks were originally established during the Depression, but still thrive today. The Salvation Army was originally formed in response to poverty and homelessness, but today reaches out into so many areas of need that it is impossible to list them all. The recent Asian tsunami that killed tens of thousands led to fundraising for similar occurrences – and this goes on unabated, years after the original disaster struck.

Everyone connected with any organization believes it to be worthy. And, of course, in a sense, this is right. Every good cause that seeks a good outcome is of value. Each one has merit and each one deserves respect.

But those that are truly successful – those that will attract donors and keep on attracting them –manage to make an emotional connection that resonates so strongly with donors that they give without question and keep on giving.

That is what all of us in charity work search for. That is what we require. That is what being worthy really means.

And to achieve it, we need to return to that equation once again:

Destiny + Process = Success

What does the equation mean? Like many things in life, it is simple on the surface, but more complex than it appears.

CHAPTER 2:
IN SEARCH OF DESTINY

The first element of the Destiny equation requires us to understand what "destiny" really is and how it applies to us.

Think of it in this way: "Destiny is a clear and unequivocal understanding of how and why that organization makes the world a better place."

You may be creating a better place for others to live, to work, to find peace of mind or joyfulness of heart. Or you may aspire to a world of freedom from illness, pain or hunger.

Your efforts may result in a world of increased spiritual comfort or salvation or physical and mental well-being for others. Alternatively, you may be growing a world of personal security and self-respect for those who have never enjoyed these qualities. You may enrich the poor, uplift the downcast, strengthen the weak or comfort the lost.

Whatever your organization does, you need to know exactly how its work improves the world.

That world may be as small as the Church you attend or the village in which you live. It may be as large as the country that you serve or a worldwide cause that you endorse and support.

No matter how large or small your "world" is, it connects you in some way with everyone else, everywhere, and makes an impact far beyond its immediate boundaries.

Your Church creates a community which impacts positively on your village or town through the example, behaviour, belief and faith of the congregation. Your foundation may help those who are bereaved. But they, in turn, will go on to help others in many different ways. Each child that your cause supports has the chance of a better life and that, in turn, makes the world a more rewarding place to live – not just for them but for many others whom they will meet in their lifetime.

The "Six Degrees of Separation" theory contends that we are all connected to each other through no more than six other people or organizations. If that is the case – and there are countless studies to support it – then your charity or cause is a vital cog in the whole wheel of life. Without it, the world is a poorer place.

However you define your connection to the rest of humanity, you need to be able to do just that: define it clearly, boldly, in terms that will resonate and connect with a variety of audiences, make sense and actually mean something. Terms that will motivate, drive and inspire all those with whom your organization comes into contact.

Destiny, to use the language of our friendly facilitator with the Good Food Group, is the **ultimate desired outcome** of the organization: the place it wants to get to so that it can ensure that it has made the world a better place.

One of the world's largest entertainment companies once stated its destiny. It is "To make people happy." An internationally acclaimed cosmetics company has one too: "To give equal opportunity to women."

One of the most famous destiny statements in the medical world is "Cancer Can Be Beaten." Another is "Give the Gift of Life." A third is "Everyone knows someone who is touched by the United Way."

It may be tempting to say that your Destiny Statement is just another fancy word for Mission Statement – and that you already have one of those. However, Mission Statements are usually statements of belief. To quote the Children's Foundation of Guelph and Wellington in Canada: "Every Child Deserves a Bright Future." This is a Mission Statement, something the Foundation truly thinks is important. But it doesn't spell out how or why the Foundation makes the world a better place.

Here's part of another Mission Statement, from one of the world's greatest and most respected universities:

"Education at (our institution) should liberate students to explore, to create, to challenge, and to lead. The support the College provides to students is a foundation upon which self-reliance and habits of lifelong learning are built: Harvard expects that the scholarship and collegiality it fosters in its students will lead them in their later lives to advance knowledge, to promote understanding, and to serve society."

You might argue that this sounds like pretty good "destiny" material. Certainly its language and intent reflect the notable work of this great institution. But is it clear how Harvard makes the world a better place? It may be implied, but it isn't unequivocal.

No, to really clarify your sense of destiny and take the first pivotal step on the road to fundraising success, you need:

The Destiny Proposition

The Destiny Proposition is tied to outcomes. It tells everyone:

- Not just what your organization does, but why it does it. To use our Children's Foundation example: "Every Child Deserves a Bright Future TO HELP THEM LIVE THAT FUTURE TO THE BENEFIT OF OTHERS."

- How its work creates a better world. For example, a Food Bank may say "Give generously to our Food Bank SO THAT HUNGER CAN BE REDUCED ONE FAMILY AT A TIME."

- Why this is important to all of us. For example, "Support carbon emission reductions now SO THAT THE WORLD CAN BREATHE CLEAN AIR FOREVER."

- Why we need to support it. Your gift to the Children's Aid Society changes lives AND STRENGTHENS FAMILIES WHO STRUGGLE.

In a sense, the Destiny Proposition is a journey that is unlikely to be completed in our lifetime. It is literally your ultimate destiny, an ideal, a transcending wish.

It is a "state of striving" to achieve an ultimate goal. People will continue to get cancer. AIDS in Africa may never be completely eliminated. No sooner will child poverty disappear in one place, but it will spring up in another. There may never be enough affordable housing for those who need it.

Yet it is equally certain that without the "state of striving," or without the enduring passion to make the world a better place, NO REAL PROGRESS will ever be made towards these and many other laudable goals.

"Everybody knows," sang Leonard Cohen, "the deal is rotten. Old Black Joe keeps picking cotton, for your ribbons and bows."

And yet there has now been a Black president in the White House and without the striving and passion of millions of people to create emancipation and put an end to formal discrimination, this might never have happened. An end to discrimination and segregation is a Destiny Proposition – it still is.

Who is to say that your Destiny Proposition is any less valid or important? The old saying, "The longest journey begins with a single step," speaks to the work of thousands of small charities, foundations and good causes. Each senior who is freed from pain; each child with a brighter future; each parent strengthened after tragic loss; each wish granted to a sick child; each abused mother restored to confidence. All of these contribute to a better world.

How to get to Your Destiny Proposition

Here are seven things that your organization needs to start THINKING and TALKING about to arrive at your Destiny Proposition. We call this:

The Passionate Proposition Process

1. **How big is the world that we impact** (the world that we can make better)?

2. **What does success look like for us in that world** (our ultimate destination)?

3. **How far away are we from achieving that success** (our challenge)?

4. **What do we have to do to close the gap** between where we are now and where we need to be (our growth and development)?

5. **Who do we need to help us** close the gap (our friends and donors)?

6. **What is our passion** that we must convey to them (success in our world)?

7. **How can we convey that passion** so that it resonates with them (our Destiny Proposition)?

Once we have answers to these questions, we need to craft the Proposition itself. Here are some suggestions to make this happen effectively:

1. **Involve a true cross-section** of your Board, staff, volunteers and current donors in this process. We call this The Destiny Conversation.

2. **Spend a reasonable amount of time discussing it**. You won't get there in a morning, but maybe in a month. Revisit it often, revise it if you need to and make it a living, breathing part of everything you do.

3. **Make every Destiny Conversation** a chance to Recognize, Respect and Reward all those who take part. The Conversation itself is part of this

Passionate Process. It reinforces, for everyone, the importance and value of doing what you do.

4. **Get some volunteer (or even paid) help** with this process. Very few groups can get there on their own without an objective facilitator to guide and direct them.

5. **Test the Destiny Proposition** with others who have not been directly involved with your organization. Does it make sense? Is it realistic? Does it motivate, inspire and create passion? Does it resonate with others?

6. **Create it and brand it.** Think of ways to integrate it into part of everything you market and promote, everything you talk about, every reason for a meeting, every decision taken.

The Destiny Proposition is the answer to the "SO THAT WHAT…?" question, as in:

- You raise money to help children who are terminally ill
  SO THAT WHAT HAPPENS?

- You give money to those who are grieving the loss of a pet
  SO THAT WHAT HAPPENS?

- You support the local environmental action group
  SO THAT WHAT HAPPENS?

The answers to the "SO THAT WHAT " questions have to make clear why your deeds, actions and gifts link whatever you do to making the world a better place. This has to be clear and unambiguous, a statement of both belief and passion, that will resonate with all those with whom your organization interacts and, ultimately – and of greatest importance – encourages people to GIVE YOU MONEY!

Ten Ways To Become Worthy

1. Have a Destiny Proposition – a clear sense of how you will positively change your world.

2. Translate this into values that underscore everything you do.

3. Make sure that everyone understands and lives those values.

4. Make the right moral decisions, even if they cause you short or long-term pain.

5. Keep your promises.

6. Do a few things consistently well and develop a reputation for them.

7. Surround your organization with people of probity, decency and good judgment.

8. Be totally transparent, even when you don't have to be.

9. Keep the best financial records possible – no shortcuts.

10. Run criminal record checks on everyone who works and volunteers with you.

CHAPTER 3:

DESTINY AND YOUR CORE VALUES

The next step in becoming truly worthy is to define your core values. What is it that makes you passionate about your organization and what you truly believe? Core values are the underpinning of all decisions and actions taken by your Board and staff and they represent a standard of behaviour – a code of conduct – that everyone who is associated with you needs to understand, to accept and, most importantly, to live by every day.

Getting to your core values isn't easy. You may be familiar with the Elevator Speech. You step into an elevator with someone you have never met who asks you what you do for a living. You have 30 seconds to get their attention, make them interested and wanting to find out more. It sounds simple, but it isn't.

Creating your core values and, even more significantly, recognizing what has to be done to LIVE them, is like that: easy on the surface, but more complex underneath.

Core values are the building blocks for a truly successful and worthy organization. Once developed, they:

- Become the litmus test against which all decisions and actions are measured. If one of your core values is "Integrity in all things," this means in practice that you always do the right thing no matter how difficult this may be for us, no matter what the consequences and "even if no-one is looking."

- Help you to recruit volunteers and staff who either live your values now, by example, or can be encouraged to adopt them with sincerity in a short time. Recruitment is always challenging. Is this person a good fit? Will he or she be a good ambassador? Selecting those who values match your own is one good way to build a great team.

- Demonstrate that you are worthy of support and generosity. If a donor asks you, "What do you believe in, what do you stand for?" and your answer is vague and ill-defined, chances are slim that the money will flow. People need to believe in you, what you represent, and what your organization thinks is important. Core values are an explicit way to express these important principles.

• Set you apart from thousands of organizations and charities that have never thought about their core values or set them down. People give to organizations and people whom they respect, with whom they feel a kinship. Donors want to know who you are, but they also want to know WHY you are. Core values express that WHY in a unique and appealing way.

All too often, people are expected to "figure out" the core values of an organization, whether they are staff, volunteers or the public at large. So articulating one's core values – having a real sense of what is truly important and valuable – is not only an excellent way to express the brand, but it helps you to be worthy in the eyes of others, with no room for misinterpretation.

Some good rules when developing core values

1. **Make them REAL.** Values can be words on a page, or they can be real. If we say "Respect for others" is a value, can we support that by the way we recognize, reward, thank and support our volunteers? How do we conduct our relationships? Do we pay our bills on time and respect our suppliers?

2. **Make them ACHIEVABLE WITH EFFORT.** Many decisions and actions arise that would be much easier to deal with if we did not have core values. But we do. Make sure we judge every decision by the litmus test question of, "Is this in line with our core values?" If the answer is "no," then the decision is probably the wrong one, no matter how "convenient" it may seem at the time.

3. **Make them INSPIRATIONAL.** Stretch and challenge Board members and volunteers to do better, to work harder, to be more aware of your cause and to be more generous simply by being their best selves at all times. Recognize, respect and reward those who consistently live the values as well as they can.

4. **MAKE THEM MEMORABLE.** People need to be able to recite them in the elevator! If they are too complicated or ponderous, no one will recall them. "Passion" is a strong and memorable word with lots of applications. "Pursuing everything we do with great passion" is a true mouthful.

5. **MAKE THEM DURABLE.** Core values do not change with the wind. They have to be able to see the organization through good times and bad, through changes and crises, through all the ups and downs of daily life. Yet, no matter what the situation, we need to be able to go back to our values to show us how to think, how to behave, how to act and react, and how to measure the ethics, morality and truth of everything we do.

All of this may seem obvious. But, consider this tale of two organizations both confronted by the same moral dilemma. Guess which one had core values that helped them to make the right decision?

The charities – both small, hard-up for cash and devoted to helping children – were offered a wonderful gift: more than $50,000 each from a local tobacco distributor who asked only that the gift be recognized with a small presentation at the organizations' next public event.

Both charities listed "commitment to wellness" as one of their core values. One of them agreed to the terms offered by the donor. The other declined the gift. The charity that accepted the funds used the money to improve its camp facilities. It rationalized the gift on the basis that the benefits of the camp would offset the negative implications of the donor's product. The other believed its core values would be compromised by accepting the gift in the first place.

There is no easy answer to these moral questions. But it is reasonably clear which one was more true to its core values, no matter what the ultimate cost.

So, how do we get to our Values?

The Values Conversation is one of the most important that any Board can conduct, yet for many it is never held.

Why?

First, because many groups find it hard to talk about these "touchy feely" things. They would rather get on with the cold, hard business of raising cash. They forget that donors only give to organizations that they perceive to be worthy and that the absence of values almost certainly translates into the absence of worthiness over time.

Second, because this is a hard conversation. It forces people to look really hard at some tough issues.

1. **Why is what we do important?** (The Destiny Proposition again) For example, we promote the principle of good manners around the world so that people will live together more tolerantly.

2. **What are our core beliefs about what we do?** For example, we believe that good manners reduce tensions and help to eliminate conflicts.

3. **What are the most important actions we take that express those beliefs best?** For example, we are consistently well-mannered in all our dealings with others and advocate strongly for good manners wherever we go.

4. **What do we expect of ourselves and others?** For example, the highest possible level of respect for other people.

5. **What behaviours must we model** with each other, with volunteers, with donors, with others? For example, the courage to challenge and change bad manners wherever we find them.

Once those fundamental questions are asked, it's important to make a list of the key values that must underpin the answers. This requires the time, energy and commitment to have the Core Values Conversation.

We recommend that you don't do this on your own, but with the help of a trained facilitator or outside moderator; someone who can help you to stay focused and on track while helping you to look as objectively as possible at the decisions you make.

Here's a typical list of potential values that might result from the questions above. Keep what works and replace the rest with words or phrases that best reflect what your organization truly believes at its core:

Compassion	**Goodness**
Hard Work	**Mercy**
Generosity	**Sharing**
Creativity	**Belief**
Participation	**Freedom**
Courage	**Equality**
Respect	**Tolerance**
Unselfishness	**Kindness**
Entrepreneurial Spirit	**Forgiveness**

Once you have a list of 15 to 20 possible Values, give it to each Board member. Ask them to do three things with it:

1. **Delete** the five that they believe most DEFINITELY do NOT apply to your organization.

2. **Then delete the next five** that PROBABLY don't apply.

3. **From the remaining 5 to10, select up to five** that most likely DO reflect what you believe you are all about.

Once each individual has his/her top five, ask them to rank them – one through five – in order of importance, with the most important being #1 and to share their lists, giving reasons for why they have selected them. Have someone keep score and compile a final list to see which values have found their way to the top.

Chances are very good that most people in the group will be reasonably consistent and a clear priority list will emerge. Here's an example of a list compiled by a small organization that provides camp placements to immigrant children in a medium-sized mid-western US town:

The Diversity Camp Foundation

CORE VALUE ANALYSIS

Core Value	Totals
Integrity	8
Respect	1
Generosity	4
Compassion	8
Teamwork	1
Commitment	7
Joy	1
Kindness	2
Family	2
Opportunity	2
Child-focused	1
Hard Work	1
Advocacy – Support	1

In this list, integrity, compassion and commitment far outstrip any other value. In fact, some that you might think would automatically rise to the top, such as child-focused, hard work or joy, rank close to the bottom of the list. This is quite interesting for an organization devoted to children!

This list demonstrates why this exercise is useful.

First, it shows what drives people to become involved. The list clearly indicates that compassion, however defined, is probably a driver of many key decisions and actions taken. When searching for new members, the Board might want to look for this trait in potential candidates.

Second, the list shows the Diversity Camp Foundation where some gaps may be. In this instance, the whole concept of being child-focused or child-centred may be weak, not necessarily the best attributes for a children's charity.

This might prompt discussions such as, "How can we learn more about the real needs of children in our community?" or, more provocatively, "How much do we actually care about children, anyway?"

The concept of "worthiness" demands that Camp Diversity asks itself these tough questions, if only to ensure that it is truly perceived to be deserving of gifts and is doing all it can to attract donors to its cause.

Finally, the list gives this charity a true building block for another equally important conversation which focuses on:

1. **Are they real, achievable, inspirational, memorable and durable**, both for us and for all others who will connect with us? For example, if a value is "commitment," does this fill us with a sense of challenge, purpose and achievement? Does it encourage all of us to "go the extra mile," work hard and do what has to be done?

2. **How are we living them on a day-to-day basis?** When have we shown these values to be true? When have we sometimes missed the boat? For

example, when we decided this year not to honor a financial commitment we made 12 months ago because the economy has since tanked, was that in line with our core value of Integrity?

3. **Do all our messages and materials reflect our values?** If so, how? If not, how can we ensure that they do? For example, should they be listed on our website, with an explanation?

4. **Does every key member of our team know what the values are**, what they mean and how to express them to others? For example, a Board member may be asked: "So, when you guys say that you practice compassion, what does that mean?" They must be able to answer the question clearly, simply and effectively.

5. **Before we implement decisions, what process can we develop** to measure all our decisions and actions against them? For example, should we have a 15-minute session at the end of each meeting to ensure that the actions we have taken are "on value"?

Values not only speak to the essential essence of a charity or cause and the people who work for it. They drive everything that the organization believes and does. In this way, they connect and resonate with potential donors who either share the same values or are transformed and motivated by them to give generously and often!

Values and the Perception Gap

One very useful tool to use when discussing values is the Perception Gap model, shown below.

THE PERCEPTION / REALITY GAP

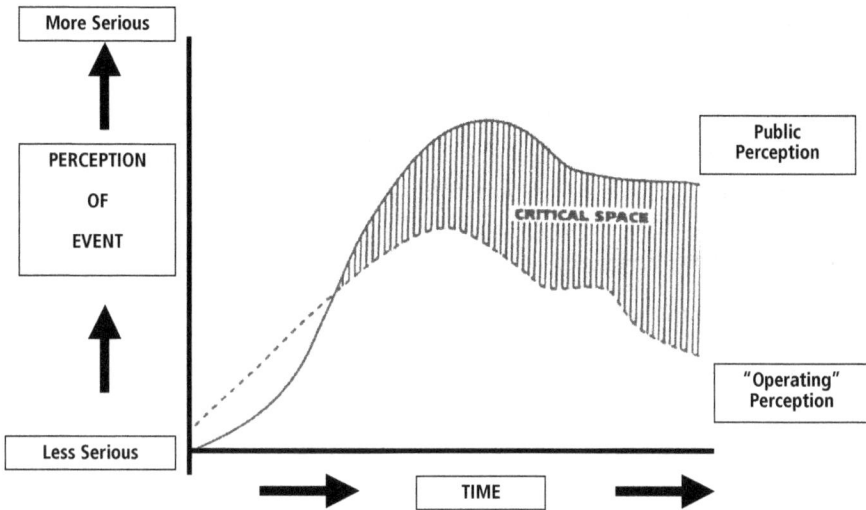

The diagram reminds us of a number of critical facts about being "worthy."

First, no matter how well run any organization is, there will always be a perception gap between what it believes it is doing and what others perceive it is doing. This is because no stakeholder, no matter how well informed, can ever have quite the same depth of knowledge and understanding about your charity as those who are involved on a daily basis.

Your job is to keep the gap between your reality and others' perceptions of that reality as narrow as possible. The smaller the gap, the higher the general level of knowledge, understanding and acceptance about you will be. The wider the gap, the greater the chance for misunderstanding, misinformation and lack of support to occur.

The "time line" in the diagram reminds us that the longer a negative perception is allowed to go unchallenged, the wider the perception gap gets and the more difficult it is to close.

Perception is fickle thing. It takes years to build up a positive perception, but it can be destroyed in a heartbeat. Alternatively, negative perceptions can be created quickly and may take many years to overcome.

Even today, more than 20 years after the event, most people associate the word "Exxon" with "oil spill" and "oil company." On the other hand, say the words "Mother Teresa," and almost everyone around the world has an immediate and positive perception of this extraordinary human being.

Secondly, stakeholder perceptions are formed in several ways:

- what they hear about you

- what they read about you

- what others say about you

- what **you** say about you

- how everyone directly involved with the charity behaves and works

- the measure of success you achieve and how you accomplish it.

This means you have to work non-stop and rigourously on managing perceptions. Everything the organization says and does should be aimed at building positive perceptions, tightening up the Gap and building goodwill.

This diagram also reminds us of several **Blinding Glimpses of the Obvious** (BGO's) in our relationships with donors and other stakeholders. Yet, because they are so obvious, many groups never consider them, or possibly worse, consider them but do nothing about them.

BGO #1: You may think that your organization is well run and worthy. But if others don't believe this is true, it isn't true

In charitable work, as in all things, perception is reality. Do you know how people think and feel about you and what have you done to find out?

BGO #2: There is a direct relationship between the Perception Gap and the amount of goodwill that you can count on when you need it. This is the Perception – Goodwill equation and looks like this:

Narrow Gap + Constant Attention = Big Goodwill Quotient

Big Gap + Lack of Attention = Small Goodwill Quotient

Any organization that takes its goodwill for granted becomes complacent. Or it fails to measure the impact of EVERYTHING that can affect its image and runs the risk of developing a Big Perception Gap in a hurry.

BGO #3: Goodwill is the most powerful component of worthiness and one that brings enormous benefits.

Those benefits are tangible, with real dollar values attached.

In his pivotal work, *Public Relations Handbook*, Philip Lesly noted that a high level of goodwill allows a successful organization to:

1. **Attract and retain top talent.** People like to be associated with something successful and the ability to attract and retain top candidates for your Board, committed volunteers and capable staff is directly related to how successful you are perceived to be. This not only gets you good people, it saves you the significant costs that come when you pick the wrong people for any job. It's also crucial to help you make your financial targets, attract top donors and maintain financial strength. A small United Way which funded about 11 agencies and programs in its community of 27,000 people had never achieved its annual fundraising target in its 38-year history. That is, until the Board persuaded the president of a well-known national company, who had recently become a resident, to take the lead. The stature, reputation, contacts and drive of the president reinvigorated

the United Way. For the next four years, it met or exceeded its targets with ease and was able to extend aid to 11 more agencies in that period.

2. **Educate and persuade others to a point of view.** If your goodwill quotient is high, so is your credibility. Your most vital need is to get people believing in you and donating to support that belief. If you manage the Perception Gap effectively, your marketing, promotion, direct mail pieces and face-to-face asks will resonate that much more effectively with stakeholders and supporters.

3. **Manage the course of change.** Change is always difficult to manage and often hard to explain. But if you do need to change your solicitation approach, your Case Statement, your involvement with donors or even your plans for the annual golf tournament, people will accept that change much more readily if they trust and respect you. A Parish Council in a suburban centre learned this when it tried to change plans for a renovation – one that long been promised to the congregation. Council members were unable to convince parishioners why long-awaited alterations to the Parish Hall and meeting rooms could not now go ahead because of funding shortfalls. It was the long-serving Pastor who helped the parishioners accept that previous promises could not be kept. Through his long term example, his faith and pastoral skills and based on the strong relationships he had built up over many years, the Pastor won the congregation over to a new point of view: that financial stability in the long term was more important than immediate and perhaps financially risky short-term renovations.

4. **Overcome errors and mistakes**. Charitable organizations are human and things do go wrong. There is no hospital in the world that has not lost a patient due to procedural error or medical mistake, nor is there a service club that hasn't messed up an event at some time or other. But once again, if your goodwill is strong and your Perception Gap is tight people will "forgive and forget" much more readily than they will if your integrity is suspect and you aren't paying attention to managing your perceptions.

5. **Attract financial support.** Donors give because they are generous. They give because your cause resonates with them. And they also give if they like being associated with you – the "feel good" factor that comes with having their money attached to something they believe has value. If your charity lacks goodwill, it also lacks perceived value – and that translates into many lost dollars that you will probably never win back.

6. **Extend lines of credit and supply.** It's often said that you cannot always manage or predict your revenues, but you can always manage your costs. One way to do that is to get better payment terms from your suppliers, extend out your payables as far as you can and gather in receivables on time and in full. These can be much more easily accomplished if you manage your perceptions with financial partners effectively and maintain that crucial reservoir of goodwill with suppliers, lenders and others.

Ten Benefits of a Great Reputation and Image

1. **Helps you to attract and retain** "the brightest and best."

2. **Acts like a magnet for donations:** people give to organizations they admire.

3. **Enables you to influence and lead change** because people trust you.

4. **Gets you "a second chance"** when you make mistakes.

5. **Allows you to extend payments** to suppliers.

6. **Gives you credibility** when trying influence behaviour change.

7. **Makes your messages more believable**.

8. **Opens doors** to potential new donors.

9. **Generates passion** for what you do and how you do it.

10. **It feels great** to be associated with a great organization.

BGO #4: If you are not living your values, your Perception Gap will suffer. In short, you need to "walk the talk" in everything you say or do on behalf of your charity so that your values are lived and expressed consistently and so that others understand and empathize with them.

Here are 5 do's and don'ts about "Living Your Values":

DO:

1. **Talk about values when recruiting staff and volunteers.** Share the values with every candidate and ask them to give you three examples from their own experience of how they have lived and expressed them.

2. **Have a sub-committee** that reviews everything your organization does from the perspective of "Is this true to our Values?" The Committee should have the power to make recommendations for change, if needed.

3. **Regularly review your values as a Board or Team.** Are they still relevant? Are they still useful? Are they helping us to make good decisions? How can we live them better?

4. **Recognize and reward** those who set a high a standard of values behaviour. They may have made a difficult moral choice or put the organization's gain above their own personal needs. They may make a significant sacrifice or supported a tough decision even though it hurt them personally. Whatever the action, it should be acknowledged.

5. **Remember the old adage that "Repetition Builds Reputation."** Values are not defined by only a few people. They need to be lived, breathed and talked about by everyone associated with your cause. Transmit the values on all publicity materials. Talk about them in public meetings. Discuss them at the Board table. Make them real and tangible and meaningful.

That way, they will define what you are all about and ensure the development of a small, tight Perception Gap that is filled with positive goodwill.

DON'T:

1. **Adopt values just because they sound good.** Everyone says that "Integrity" is a value because it sounds like the right thing to do. But if you aren't truly sure what it means to you, don't list it. Instead, list something that does make sense, like "Honesty in all things."

2. **Look for a quick fix by borrowing the values of another group.** There is no shortcut to the hard work required to have values that are truly valid for your group and that will help you achieve what you need.

3. **Let emotions or friendship get in the way of good judgment,** especially when recruiting staff or volunteers. A close friend may not necessarily have or share the values that you need. That doesn't make them bad people. But it does make them suspect in their value to you. Be hard-hearted and pragmatic about picking the right people for the right jobs. Your future depends on it.

4. **Post the values and forget about them** (See Do's # 2 and 3 above!).

5. **Abandon values when they get in the way.** There will be many times when an easy way out looks good. But if any decision contradicts or flies in the face of values, it is almost always the wrong one. Test each decision with a simple question: Is this "on value" or "off-value"? Then, make the right choice.

Values are one of those things that many organizations think of as nice to have but not that important. Dead wrong. Values are the MOST IMPORTANT foundation upon which an organization is built. They:

1. **Define** who and what you are.

2. **Give** you standards of thought, word and deed to follow consistently.

3. **Provide** common terms of reference for all those with who you interact.

4. **Help** you to measure the validity of everything you do.

5. **Give** you vital tools with which to manage your Perception Gap.

6. **Create** a reservoir of goodwill that you can draw on for many reasons, not the least of which is encouraging other people to give you money!

Five things to think about Values

1. If asked, can I give examples of how I try to live them every day?

2. Do I live them even when it's inconvenient?

3. I may be disesteemed because of them. Is this OK?

4. Will I stand up and be counted for them when I need to be?

5. Am I trying to make a positive difference because of them?

CHAPTER 4:

BECOMING WORTHY BY ASSOCIATION

When the Board members of the Good Food Group (GFG) met that Saturday morning and confronted the harsh reality that their Executive Director did not feel qualified to fundraise, they had to take a hard look at themselves as well.

How many of them had fundraising experience? It was true that most of them had been involved in charity dances, golf tournaments or bingo drives over the years. But few had real experience in raising hundreds of thousands of dollars over a sustained period of time.

How many of them had real money to donate, or, at the very least, were connected to where the real money was in the community? Again, most of them had painstakingly built up their pensions and savings and could be said to be "people of means." But there is a world of difference between "people of means" and "people who can truly donate large amounts."

Finally, how many had ever asked others to donate large or significant amounts or could challenge others to match what they themselves were giving?

The answer, in all cases, was "none." When it came to the crunch, not one of the Board members had the experience to raise big dollars, the financial resources required to give a large amount themselves or to ask others to do likewise.

In this, they were failing the organization they cared so much about. This was not intentional and certainly not due to any action they were taking. They were failing because the main reason that their Board existed was to raise money.

The main reason that almost ANY Board of a small charity exists is, ABOVE ALL, to raise money for that organization.

The Good Food Group's board cared passionately about the REASON they needed money: they cared for the cause. But a good cause without support is a hollow shell and will not last long. Fundraising is crucial to success. A Board that cannot deliver that success, in spite of all its great intentions, will never achieve what it really wants to do.

In this, the GFG was not alone. In fact, most Boards of Directors of smaller charitable organizations, while they are respected, established and recognized for their good work, tend not to have what is often called "real money" and are not that skilled at raising funds.

Ten Attributes of a Good Board Member

1. Demonstrates passion for what you do and how you do it.

2. Knows the goals of the organization.

3. Has influence in one or more sectors of your community.

4. Has the time and energy to give what it takes.

5. Puts the organization first and his/her ego last.

6. Attends and participates at all meetings.

7. Is always prepared.

8. Is honest, transparent and forthright in all things.

9. Works hard but still has fun.

10. Gives whatever funds s/he can, whenever asked.

Small charities may not wish to admit this, but one of the FIRST things a potential donor does when approached for funds is check the Board of Directors and ask:

• Do I know anyone on this Board?

• Are they reputable, respected, well-established, or connected?

• Do I mix with them socially or know people that do?

• Do their values represent my values?

• Are they worthy of my support?

That's what "Worthy by Association" means. Donors need and want to associate in some way with the people who drive the bus. It's a known fact in fundraising that peers give to peers or FOR peers. And if potential donors have no one on the Board that they consider a peer, the Board will become the reason that the charity is unworthy of their support.

That isn't to say that the board of the GFG, or any other organization for that matter, cannot hope to attract real dollars. People give for all kinds of reasons, not least of which is that they support and believe in the Destiny Proposition we discussed earlier.

Big donors MAY give because they admire a priest, a doctor, a community-minded citizen or an athlete on the Board. They WILL give if they have a direct, or indirect, personal association with individuals around the table.

The GFG board is not somehow second-class or imperfect because its members do not have real connections to the money in the community. Boards need people with good hearts, generous character, a will to succeed, a capacity for hard work and, above all, a passion for their cause. Anyone from any walk of life, regardless of socio-economic status, belief, background or financial standing can be an outstanding Board member. Charities all over the world are led by such Board members.

But, let's be honest – it helps if some, or all of them – are well-enough connected and established to attract the big dollars in the community.

Having those connections adds a new dimension to their capacity to raise funds. It makes them more worthy of support.

How are most Boards formed? Here are the five of the most common Board member "types." See how many of them apply to your Board members.

Five reasons that people join Boards

1. **The PASSIONATE**: They have direct personal experience of the cause. Seven of the ten Board members of a bereavement support group had lost a child. Many associated with alcohol recovery groups have been touched by addiction in some way. Universally, every Church council is made up of believers. Board members in this case bring a very personal passion and drive to the organization and usually give extensive time and energy to it.

2. **THE INTERESTED:** These members expressed an interest and were asked to join. It is estimated that over 50% of all Boards are predominantly made up of those looking for a worthwhile cause and an invitation to assist. All are welcomed, but how many are truly right for the Board and/or its cause?

3. **THE SPOTLIGHT SEEKERS:** These folk want to pad their resume. Sadly, this happens far too often. People join Boards that they believe are high-profile and bask in the recognition that this gives them. At one very large metropolitan YMCA, a senior-ranking community industrialist joined the Board. Everyone else was delighted, as they would finally become "worthy by association" to those with money. But after 12 months, the Board member made one meeting, and that was via conference call. He took up space and did little else.

4. **THE PROFESSIONAL:** They have a special skill set. Many Boards have a doctor, lawyer, accountant or human resource specialist on their team.

Marketers are also in high demand. Many are asked to offer their personal expertise for free and do so willingly. In fact, many would usually rather contribute skills and talents other than their professional area of expertise. They often become tired or bored, or both, and may not be effective.

5. **THE COLLECTOR:** They collect Boards like butterflies. These folk are usually retired and anxious to remain relevant and make a contribution (and many do). All too often, however, they over-extend or are not truly able to focus on the main cause because they have so many other irons in the fire.

Let's face it, if these good people did not exist, there would be very few Boards. You may be part of an organization whose Board is made up entirely of these five types and be very successful.

But the critical question when it comes to fundraising is:

"Can this Board put money on the table – or bring other people's money to the table?"

Or,

"Can this group connect with and be worthy to other people who can put money on the table?"

If the answer to these questions is NO, you need to re-think the composition of the Board to achieve these ends.

Four Ways to Build a Worthy Board

1. **Maintain the Passion:** You absolutely need to have those who are passionate for the cause. While they may not have funds, they can tell the story, inspire and motivate others, lead by example and model behaviours for volunteers and donors. We think 40% of your Board should be made up of "passionates."

2. **Build "Street Cred":** Invite one or two with a clear track record of success in similar organizations. A very successful children's charity in a southeastern community reached out to a local National Hockey League referee. He had done brilliant work to acquire substantial silent auction prizes for many charitable events. He brought that skill and talent to the new Board, and everyone prospered. We suggest that 15% of your Board should have some "street cred."

3. **Connect to the Money:** At least 10% of your Board should be people of means or extremely well-connected – by blood or bonding – to those who have money in the community. These folk are the ones who will be able to lead the big Campaign, or get someone else to do it. They can make the upfront donation and also make the big asks. Those who have money also know where it is "hidden" in the community. As any fundraiser knows, the visible money is only a tiny fragment of the real wealth that lurks beneath the surface. And, it is a lot harder to say "no" to someone of real wealth and worth who has already put money on the table, than it is to someone who means well but is not "worthy" in the true sense of the word. So follow the money!

4. **Get Worker Bees:** The balance of your Board – about 35% – can be the "interesteds" who are committed to working hard and who are absolutely essential for any Board, whether governance or operational. They can be drawn from all walks of life and all backgrounds and, when used to best advantage, are the "eyes and ears" of the Board in the community. This group can contain the professionals with specific skills you may need, or be made up of anyone with a good heart and a willingness to spend the time. Don't ignore the worker bees!

44 – WORTHY AND PREPARED

There are no shortcuts!

The principle of bringing the right people to the Board table is vital, even if you have a cause that seems to be so compelling that it will sell itself.

This is especially true if you are asking people to donate to religious, child-focused or political campaigns. These issues evoke great passion, and it is easy to think that passion alone will drive donors to give, and to do so generously.

Nothing could be further from the truth. In fact, those causes that are linked to the universal benefit of mankind still need to make sure that they have the right people connected to them, in the right way, before real money will flow. The perceived benefits of the cause, alone, will not do the job.

Consider this cautionary tale of a famous Catholic boys' school, which had been operating for more than 100 years. In its day, it had nurtured hundreds of students who went on to fame and fortune in later life, many of whom credited the school with their success. The school was not only famous for its faith and its academics. It also enjoyed one of the most prominent sports programs in the country and leading athletes regularly spoke of their playing days at the school as the foundation of later triumphs. Its list of high-achieving alumni was long and impressive. History, reputation and money were all on its side.

On the surface, raising money for the school should have been easy.

So, when it went into a capital campaign hoping to raise $7,000,000 for school expansion and modernization, the priests in charge and their closest lay volunteer advisers were more than confident that the target could be reached without much effort.

They decided to use a tried and true method of religious-based fundraising: find wealthy individuals and alumni and ask them for donations. These people, they reasoned, would feel compelled to give because of the unique connection they had with the school and the church. In fact, they were so confident that they could raise the funds that they decided that it was unnecessary to do any more than that.

They did not need to have a worthy Board. In fact, even though they had several Board members who were exceptionally worthy by association, they chose not to use them in the campaign.

They also decided against using professional help. In fact, when it was offered by a skilled alumnus, they shunned it. They didn't feel that they needed to spend money to reach their goal: those associated with the cause through their history or their faith would provide support.

What the campaign team did not take into account were changing attitudes towards religion. A study undertaken in the U.S. in the 1990s (published around the time of the campaign) showed that 85% of self-identified Catholics who went to church regularly did not believe in some of the most fundamental assumptions of their church – such as the infallibility of the Pope or even all of the 10 Commandments. Most regular church-goers attended for the sense of community or the experience.

As well, it had been common practice for some time at the school to accept public funds during a time when the expansion and public funding of a separate Catholic school system became public policy. Although the school was now wholly private, many younger alumni had only experienced it as a semi-public institution. They did not share the entrepreneurial spirit that a totally private school often fosters, and did not understand that the school, no longer able to tap public funds, could not easily access them again.

Finally, the school had done little to extend its reach beyond a core group of alumni who made it a point to stay connected with the institution. There was little outreach to alumni of any generation. The school's database was 50% inaccurate. Many of the addresses were for the parents of former students, not the individuals themselves.

Notwithstanding these obvious problems – ones that advisors or professionals would have pointed out immediately – the campaign team pushed on, thinking that the organization's long history, stellar reputation and links to its core audience would bring success.

What happened was an entirely different outcome. Since no professionals in campaign operations were involved with the program, it was rolled out incorrectly both from a timing and promotional point of view.

No worthy Board members were used to identify, cultivate and ask major donors for support, so no gifts were secured before the public announcement of the campaign. There was general indifference to the case for support and to the campaign leaders, none of whom were the "right people" playing the "right role."

Some alumni provided small gifts, which because of the lack of sophistication of the campaign team, were recognized at too high a level. Most campaigns of $7,000,000 would likely need two or three lead gifts of $1,000,000 or more, secured very early in the process. The school did none of the groundwork, and instead began to announce the small four- and five-figure gifts as though they were transformational.

The campaign was also unprepared for the lack of overall response from business and community leaders who identified themselves as Catholic and had the means to provide large donations. These individuals had long been identified and cultivated by various other Catholic and secular institutions, and had given them significant support. When presented with the case by the lead volunteers, they did not respond with the gifts that the school so badly needed. Why did this happen?

The question most potential donors asked was very straightforward: "Why should I donate to the school when I didn't attend the school myself and none of my children or grandchildren attends? What is the compelling case?"

The answer was simply that they were Catholic and that this was a Catholic cause. But this completely failed to resonate with the prospective supporters. The people making the ask were not the right people. The case was poorly defined. The assumption that faith alone would carry the day was sadly misplaced. The Board – and thus, the school – no longer had the stature it perceived it had enjoyed in the past. The association of the cause was not enough to ensure success.

The lessons here are clear:

1. **Take nothing and no one for granted.** You need to get the right Board and the best leadership for your campaign. Reputation, good works and fine sentiments will not raise the funds you need.

2. **Your past success guarantees you nothing in the future.** Every campaign or fundraising event is a new beginning, a stand alone activity. Relying on what worked before will probably not get the job done. Cruising on your reputation certainly won't.

3. **Who you know – and who knows about you** – is still essential for success. Work your relationships and get the very best Board that you can!

Eight Ways to Keep Your Board Energized

1. ENERGY EXERCISE: Once a month, sit down for 20 minutes and list all the things – large or small – you have done well the month before.

2. BENEFITS EXERCISE: Go around the table and ask all Board members to list 2-3 ways in which the organization has changed their lives for the better.

3. THANKS TO YOU: Say Thank You to Board members who go "over and above." Write It Too!

4. TELL STORIES: Invite those who benefit from your work to come and tell their stories at the Board table. It makes your work real!

5. BROADEN HORIZONS: Provide education and orientation sessions that build skills and expand minds.

6. TEAM BUILDING: Practice team building exercises that are fun and useful.

7. ROTATE TASKS: Ensure that every Board member regularly takes on different aspects of your work.

8. Have fun – a party, dinner or outing does wonders for morale.

CHAPTER 5:
THE WORTHINESS OF VOLUNTEERS

While your Board needs to reflect worthiness, your volunteer group also plays a hugely significant role in attracting the support of potential donors.

Many of the best-run organizations use their volunteer base, in part, as a training ground for future Board members. Someone whom you really want to be part of your team may not have the time or inclination to be a Board member – yet. But many will agree to sign on as volunteers, even in a cameo role on one committee. You should grab onto this enthusiasm with both hands and take full advantage of it.

Selecting great volunteers is as important as picking the right Board members. While many may offer to help, not everyone may necessarily be a "good fit." You will get some volunteers who mean well but do little. Or you'll get some who do a lot but do it poorly. On the other hand, the right volunteers will not only bring energy, passion, skills and varied experience to your cause, they will also serve as your very best brand ambassadors.

Assume each volunteer knows 100 people in a community very well. That doesn't seem like many, but it is probably close to the mark. (Think about your own intimate contact list of friends, key business associates, family and neighbours. It is rare that your list will exceed 100 people).

If you have 10 great volunteers each with 100 contacts, that's 1,000 people in the community that can learn more about you from your ambassadors.

Now assume that each of those 1,000 people can be persuaded to give $10 a year to you. That's $10,000 and you have barely scratched the surface of their potential giving. If you extend this still further, and assume that each of the 1,000 also know 100 people, then the opportunity to bring in real money just by managing that initial group of volunteers effectively becomes almost limitless.

Of course, this only works if the volunteers are passionate about the organization, fully understand its mandate and know its story. Armed with those three ingredients, a good volunteer can literally be worth his or her weight in gold because they can connect to the gold!

The Six Degrees of Separation Theory we mentioned earlier says that only six personal contact points separate us from anyone else we wish to reach on the planet. So if we need to make personal (not technological) contact with a tribal chieftain in a small African village, we can do so by working out who can first help us to get closer. This person then does the same thing with some one else, and so on, until the required contact is made.

In today's world of Google, FaceBook, Twitter, Skype and other social media, it has certainly become easier to find anyone, anywhere. But to make personal contact – which is so essential in fundraising – the old theory still works well.

This means that your network of volunteers is probably able to bring you and your cause into contact with any member of the community you need to reach.

And that, in itself, is a BGO (Blinding Glimpse of the Obvious). In fact, we'll call it BGO #5:

BGO #5: Your Volunteers can connect you to the money but first you need to truly connect with your volunteers!

There are literally hundreds of excellent courses in how to recruit and manage Worthy Volunteers. Here are 10 of the best points to remember:

10 Ways to Find Worthy Volunteers

1. **Identify your gaps.** Don't just say, "We need volunteers." Instead, clearly identify those areas where you most in need support and help and decide what type of volunteer will best help you to fill that need.

2. **Establish criteria.** Make a list of the ten most valuable characteristics that each of your volunteers should have in order to be "right" for your organization. This list should probably include the need to be passionate about your cause, to have sufficient time, to be a hard worker and so on.

Use the list rigorously when assessing whether a potential volunteer can really help you or not.

3. **Create a volunteer management plan.** You should have a clear strategy for how volunteers are recruited, trained and deployed in your organization. Our natural tendency is to select anyone who says, "I'd like to be a volunteer," but this is not always productive. Volunteers are like a reserve army: they need to be educated, helped, trained and given the proper resources to do the job you want them to do.

4. **Create a sense of team.** Volunteers like to know that they are part of a larger organization, so practice effective team-building techniques, just as you might for your staff at work or for the local baseball team that you coach. Team-building creates unity, a sense of common purpose, and it motivates and energizes volunteers almost more than anything else you can do.

5. **Keep volunteers informed.** People like to know how their efforts are paying off in terms of results, so make sure that volunteers know how well each event has done, where it succeeded, where it might have done better and to what extent their efforts contributed to the final end result. It has been said that you cannot ever communicate too much with volunteers. The more they hear from you, the more they feel part of the team, and the harder they will work for you all the time.

6. **Evaluate effort.** While it may not be fair to hold volunteers to the same standard of excellence expected from fellow workers, volunteers need to be evaluated occasionally and, if necessary, helped to improve if this will contribute to the results you want to achieve.

7. **Recognize and reward.** No matter how modest they may be, everyone likes to be recognized for the contribution they have made. So make sure you recognize all volunteers regularly, provide them with small tokens of thanks and appreciation, and publicize and promote to their names in all appropriate ways, whenever you can.

8. **Be consistent with messaging.** Develop a series of three or four key messages about the organization that you use consistently when communicating with volunteers. These might focus on your fundraising goals, your strategic priorities, your need for innovation and creativity, your vision of the future, and so on. Encourage all volunteers to use these key messages whenever they communicate with others about your work. Most importantly, ensure that every volunteer clearly understands what your organization does, whom it serves and how it carries out its mission. Earlier, we mentioned the "elevator speech." Your volunteers need to be able to repeat your elevator speech so that everyone they meet immediately says, "I'd like to be a part of that organization!"

9. **Don't let volunteers become isolated in "silos."** Other people will expect your volunteers to know almost everything about your organization, even if they only help out with one small event or activity. So make sure every volunteer at least has a working knowledge of the big picture – a quick overview of everything you do, not just the event with which he or she may be associated.

10. **Recruit constantly.** Volunteers come and go just like employees in any company. Make sure that every member of your Board, for example, is constantly looking for potential new recruits. You may want to give each Board member a target to find two or three volunteers each month. Or, you can team up with the local volunteer centre to send you the names of potential applicants on a regular basis.

No matter how you recruit your volunteers, each one of them will only join you if they believe in your cause, believe in the way you conduct your enterprise, have respect for your board members and recognize the value of everything you do.

In other words, they will only join you if they believe you to be worthy. In exchange, they will enhance your image and reputation in the community by the way they represent you, work for you and act as unpaid ambassadors for your brand.

THE VOLUNTEER LOYALTY LADDER

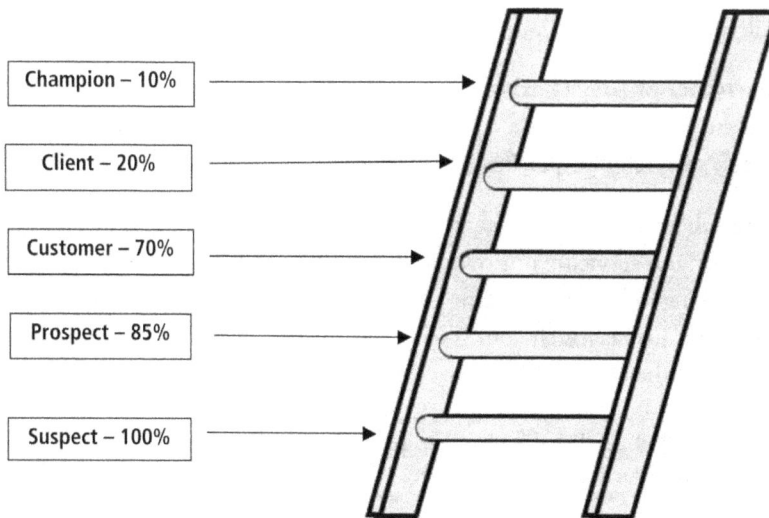

Champion – 10%

Client – 20%

Customer – 70%

Prospect – 85%

Suspect – 100%

How can we build volunteer satisfaction and service at every level of this ladder?

The Loyalty Ladder has been around for years as a way of helping businesses to categorize their customers and to create ways to connect with them at every rung of the ladder.

Very few organizations use it as a way of recruiting and keeping volunteers. Yet it offers as many practical suggestions and tips for building brand ambassadors and workers as it does for finding and keeping customers. The techniques are very similar.

When using the ladder, keep in mind two very important principles of customer service that apply equally to your relationship with volunteers (as well as all your stakeholders):

1. **The customer of your charity is "everyone but me."** In other words, every person with whom you come into contact is a potential ally, donor, volunteer, storyteller or perception manager for your brand.

2. **"We are our own first customers."** We need to do the best possible job of working for and servicing our own staff, Board and volunteers if we want them to do a good job of servicing others. The person in the office cubicle next to you is just as much your "customer" as the donor who wants to be recognized for her generosity.

Let's take a look at each rung and realize how powerful the Loyalty Ladder is as an idea generator for building strong relationships with volunteers and others.

"Suspects" is the term used for all those volunteers who come into contact with an organization for the **very first time**. Think of them like shoppers in a retail store who are checking out the merchandise. When a clerk offers to help, the shopper may say "No thanks, I am just looking around." Similarly, potential volunteers who may be interested in your organization are first going to check you out.

We call these initial contacts "Moments of Truth," the moment when a first positive or negative impression is formed. Many of these first impressions are created around the initial point of contact. These may include your voicemail, the image of your logo, a chance encounter with another volunteer, something that is read about you in the media, or simply the look of your building or delivery van.

It is vital to manage these Moments of Truth effectively if you want to be successful in recruiting volunteers. In business, there are many excellent examples of organizations that have built their reputation almost entirely on managing the Moments of Truth well. The Four Seasons Hotel chain, for example, is recognized around the world for its first-class service. It has created a culture where every single employee is constantly aware of how impressions may be created and they do their best to ensure that those impressions are positive, all the time.

So take a good hard look at every potential point of contact for a new volunteer. Is your signage clean and visible? Is it your voicemail welcoming and clear? Is the reception area clean and tidy and does the receptionist greet people warmly and effectively? How positive is your media coverage and is your marketing reflecting the kind of organization that you are? Most importantly, do all staff and volunteers voice the key messages about your organization consistently and clearly? Is everyone speaking with the same voice and giving off the same messages?

One of the biggest mistakes many organizations make is failing to follow up quickly and effectively once a potential volunteer indicates interest. How quickly you respond to this first contact is a sure indication of how valuable you perceive your volunteers to be. You need to make contact quickly.

A quick look at the Loyalty Ladder shows that if you manage your Moments of Truth effectively, you should be able to encourage about 85% of potential volunteers to take the next step by becoming a "prospect."

"Prospect" is the term used for those people who liked their first impression and now want to know more. Their initial feeling that you are a worthy organization needs to be reinforced by many factors including the quality of your marketing materials, your website, the way in which you introduce them to your services and the welcome they receive from other volunteers.

It is said that people manage "suspects," while materials and resources manage "prospects."

As we shall see in the "Prepared" section of this book, it is essential to have good protocols and policies in place for the orientation, training and development of new volunteers. You also need good materials and resources in place to help them to learn as much as possible about you in a short period of time.

Consider the situation if someone asks you for a business card and you don't have one. Your colleague may not show it, but there is just a tinge of disappointment, of being let down that you did not have this most basic of marketing tools at the ready.

The same is true when volunteers or donors want to know more. If you have no "more" to give them, or it is not very effective, the chances that they will slip away are significantly increased.

If you are able to react quickly and if the materials and information you provide about your organization are effective, almost 70% of the initial suspects may end up as very effective volunteers for your cause.

We call this 70% the "Transactors" group. Transactors are the lifeblood of any organization. They are the ones who willingly show up to help at any event. They sell refreshments, stuff envelopes, assist with the setup of tables and chairs, plan the fundraising dance, make phone calls and do all of the hundred-and-one chores that are so vital to the effective operation of any charitable cause. Without them and without the skills and talents that they bring to the table, most organizations will perish very quickly.

With our Transactors we use the phrase, "Repetition builds reputation." By this, we mean that we need to treat our volunteers with consistency. We need to be careful not to overload them, to thank them, to recognize them, to ensure that their contribution is noted and publicized and share the results of their work with them.

If we can continue with this "repetition," we will rapidly earn a reputation for being a great place to volunteer. Those who join us will do so because they think we are worthy of the time, effort and commitment that they have given to us. If we fail to do these small but important things consistently and well, we will rapidly become unworthy. Volunteers will leave us in droves.

So take a close look at the day-to-day treatment of your current volunteers. Are they being given fulfilling and rewarding things to do? Are they made to feel special? Do they have a clear understanding of your mission, mandate and values? Are they able to articulate and convey the key messages about your charity to donors, influencers, community leaders and partners?

Take a closer look at the volunteers themselves. Harsh though it may seem, volunteers are a little like the animals in George Orwell's book *Animal Farm*. They are all equal, but some are more equal than others. There are some volunteers, perhaps 20% of the original number of suspects that first came into your orbit, who can do considerably more for your organization than move chairs or sell raffle tickets.

We call these volunteers the "Client" group. Clients are special, because they have either power or influence in the wider community in which you need to do business. They may have significant resources themselves, or have access to others who do. They are generally thought of as community leaders – either in business, the arts, politics or philanthropy – or just by reputation.

Clients are the group members who can help you achieve your financial targets, perhaps more effectively than almost any other volunteer group. What's more, they demonstrate an interest in what you do and how you do it that goes beyond mere volunteering. They want to participate actively and constructively in helping you grow and become successful.

The phrase we use here is the "Care and Feeding of Clients." This group needs special attention, such as access to information about the organization that others may not have, an opportunity to participate in strategy sessions, the chance to serve in a leadership capacity or in high-profile volunteering opportunities that make them feel that they are important members of your team.

It is important to recognize that Clients do not necessarily have to be wealthy. Nor do they need to be mature or advanced in years. What they need to be is powerful or influential. The leader of the student council at your local university may be influential because she can connect with young people. Similarly, a volunteer whose profession takes her into many businesses may also be influential, because of the number of contacts that she can make for you. If you look at your database of volunteers, you should be able to check off a significant number who are clearly influential.

Clients with power are usually easier to identify. Obviously, the largest employer in your community has power – and probably significant influence as well. The Mayor has power. So do the leaders of the major service clubs or the chairman of a prominent foundation or charitable group who may be able to give you assistance. The University President has power. So does the Executive Director of the United Way.

Again, your volunteer list may surprise you with the number of people it contains who are "powerful."

From this group, we can identify a final team of volunteers who are right at the top of the food chain. These are your "Champions." Champions are identified as being those who take an active pleasure and enjoyment from promoting and helping your organization in every way that they can.

They may give significant sums of money themselves or encourage others to do the same. They may help you open up relationships that you could not otherwise cultivate on your own. They can be powerful resources when it comes to recruiting other volunteers. They provide sound strategic advice and guidance. They may bring very special skills to the table: business acumen, philanthropic connections, political clout, the ability to speak well in public and the ability to be great ambassadors for your brand.

Just as your Clients require special care and attention, your Champions must be even more fully integrated into all of your fundraising efforts. They may require confidential updates on activities, small and intimate dinners where you lay out your strategic plans, one-on-one conversations to solicit their ideas and the very best recognition awards that you can give them to demonstrate their contribution to your organization.

Obviously, every single one of your volunteers needs to be thanked, appreciated and recognized for the work that they do. But take a good hard look at your volunteer list and start to segment them according to the Loyalty Ladder. By binding to them right at the "Suspect" and" Prospect" levels you can create a solid base from which to fill any volunteering need.

By identifying your volunteers as Transactors, Clients or Champions, you can determine the amount of time, resources and energy that must be directed to each particular group to give you the maximum return you need from every single volunteer.

New Blood Brings New Energy!

Here is a great example of how new volunteer blood completely transformed a large community hospital's sense of worthiness and ability to raise money.

The hospital had always been an important asset to its community, dating back to when the town was a key port on the Great Lakes. As the community changed from being a small farming and marina town to a large recreational and retirement centre, the hospital felt the pressure of increased demand for health services.

The hospital asked its foundation to provide increased levels of funding so that much-needed equipment could be purchased. At that time, the foundation's volunteer group was made up almost entirely of truly local (born and raised) individuals. Their passion for the hospital was real, but their fundraising skills had not evolved. This volunteer group continued to look at the traditional community for support, but their effort was insufficient to meet the new and ever-increasing demands of the hospital. Local contacts using traditional means of fundraising simply could not meet the required goals.

Over the next four years, as the hospital continued to struggle with funding issues, the makeup of the foundation's volunteer group changed dramatically. It went from one dominated by the local community to one that featured many new residents – mostly transplanted professionals from the very large metropolitan area nearby. They came with the experience of serving on fundraising boards that had consistently raised large sums of money from the community.

The inclusion of this new blood into the volunteer group galvanized the foundation. It enabled it to focus to a much greater degree on the new wealth that had moved – permanently or seasonally – to the community. This immediately generated significantly more fundraising dollars and enabled the foundation to meet the growing needs of the hospital. It also provided relief for the hardworking and well-intentioned local community members who had faithfully supported the hospital for so many years.

Learning from the Donkeys

Consider also the case of The Donkey Sanctuary of Canada. As its name suggests, the organization is a sanctuary for unwanted donkeys. There is a long and well-recorded history of abuse towards this animal; this is well-known in the equine community and amongst those who are knowledgeable about animal welfare issues. The donkey also has a very strong place in religious tradition as the animal that carried Jesus into Jerusalem the week before his death on the Cross. Preventing their abuse stirs considerable passion in many donors, even among those who may not own or know much about donkeys.

The Donkey Sanctuary started by accident. A family in an agricultural community, who were long-time animal lovers, was asked by a friend to house an unwanted donkey in an unused stable. They agreed. Within a week, they had a call from someone else wondering if they wanted to take additional animals. The owners agreed again. Shortly after that, another call was received, and then another. The sanctuary was born.

As is the case with most animal rescue operations, the sanctuary is costly to run. The animals need to be housed and there are significant feeding and medical expenses. The founding family quickly realized two things. Firstly, that the name of the sanctuary was its mission and, secondly, that its mission was one that a core group of passionate people would probably find very worthy. Cash donations, as a result, have always been relatively easy to secure.

The family has also never had difficulties in finding volunteer support. The plight of the animals, the fact that they are helpless and harmless and yet still subject to abuse, stirs both great sadness and great generosity in many people. The founders have built the sanctuary almost entirely through the efforts of a core volunteer group whom they nurture, recognize and reward consistently well. They have been careful never to step too far beyond their original mandate, aside from taking in some related animals, such as mules. They have not diversified or branched out into other forms of animal welfare. This allows the volunteer group to remain focused and fully committed to the task at hand.

Because it has remained true to its niche and managed its volunteer base exceptionally well, The Donkey Sanctuary has remained top of mind and worthy, for all those who support it.

CHAPTER 6:

BECOMING WORTHY BY DEFAULT

Another critical yet often unrecognized way of becoming worthy, is to be what's known as "worthy by default."

This occurs when your cause is so universal, and is experienced by so many people in so many different ways, that it becomes almost a natural reflex to donate to it whenever the opportunity arises. Cancer is, sadly, so widespread that almost every family has been touched by it in one way or another, often prompting people to give because of that direct association with someone whom they know or love.

Other illnesses often encourage the same level of generosity. Organizations that combat the effects of heart disease, Alzheimer's disease, Parkinson's and Lou Gehrig's Disease (ALS) all benefit from a collective recognition of how significantly these diseases affect the global community.

Each year, for example, the American and Canadian cancer societies receive large donations through estate gifts. They consider this to be an important part of their fundraising process and they have the wide reach and a well-staffed office to deal with these gifts effectively. Many estate gifts come from people who have never donated to them before. Why?

Partly, these societies believe, that because they are recognized as well-managed organizations, which carefully steward the funds that they receive. I think this paragraph needs to be clarified Are you saying that because the society sees themselves as well managed so people give to them?

But when digging deeper, the societies also recognize that the majority of their estates gifts come from people whose lives have been taken by cancer. Their cause is deemed worthy because the donors are either suffering from cancer themselves or know someone who has experienced it.

Similarly, the John Howard Society, which is noted for its great work in helping former prisoners to re-enter society, is automatically deemed worthy by all individuals and families who have experienced the prison experience – either directly or by association with someone else.

Mothers Against Drunk Driving (MADD) can trace its success to the fact that a significant portion of the population – whether through a loved one, a friend or a community member – has been touched in some way by this significant criminal activity. The organization can rely on this "emotion by association" to generate significant funds without a corresponding outlay of promotional or marketing effort. It also reaches out to the community in general to reinforce this emotional connection through its messaging and advertising.

And many have at some time been involved in a hospice relationship, or know of someone close to us who has. Once again, hospices can rely on a long-term level of support from those who have had relatives or friends pass away in a gentle, caring hospice environment. Our automatic "default" emotions of love, compassion, sadness and grief in the presence of death, contribute significantly to our desire to see hospices survive and expand their services wherever possible.

So, tell your story in a worthy way

Your organization may not the able to generate that same "default" response. But, it is possible for you to tell you a story in such a compelling way that many potential donors will feel connected to you even if they have never ever had a personal experience of the work that you do. Charities that are involved in fighting child abuse children or that support children who have been abused, often find that by telling real life stories from real life people to potential donors, they can trigger the giving response. Almost everyone can relate to the pain that child abuse causes, even if they have never directly experienced it themselves.

Similarly, organizations that enable children to play sports or recreational activities that might otherwise be denied them because of lack of funds, often receive donations from many affluent parents. While they can pay for their own child's sports programs, they also relate to the benefits that sports bring to children – notably disadvantaged children – and want to make sure they do not miss out on the experience.

Organizations who deal with the care and safety of "at-risk" senior citizens often find that they can tell such a compelling story about the tragedy and sadness of senior abuse, that many people are driven to give, even if they have never witnessed this behaviour themselves. Almost all of us, after all, know someone who is elderly, frail and vulnerable.

So, take a good hard look at whether or not you may be "worthy by default." Is your cause one that almost everyone can relate to, in one way or another? If not, you need to try and change the conversation about it, and change the key messages you are using. By positioning your brand so that it has a more universal appeal, you can generate greater support for your cause.

Make the emotional connection

You can never assume worthiness by default. You may have a cause that touches millions every day, but unless you reach out and connect with them at the right emotional level, being worthy by default alone will only take you so far.

Paul Newman's famous movie *Cool Hand Luke* contains the equally famous line, "What we have here, is a failure to communicate." This message has been used by many organizations over the years to explain their lack of success in making contact with the marketplace. The inference is always "If we could communicate better, we would do better."

In fact, there has always been plenty of communication going on. Today, with modern technology, one could argue that there is far too much "communication." Much of it is poorly planned, poorly structured and poorly transmitted. It is estimated that the volume of communicated information doubles every five years. But human beings have not yet developed the capacity to absorb all of this communication, so a great deal of it is simply tuned out and ignored.

So there is no failure of "communication." Instead, there is a failure of "connection." If we are worthy by default but not getting the funds that we should, it may be because we are not connecting effectively with the right people, using the right message, at the right time, and in the right way.

By "connection," we mean being able to stir the emotions: love, compassion, pity, generosity, concern, and even the negative emotions such as fear or guilt. We need to be able to reach out and tell a story that truly connects with the emotions of those who can give us financial help.

Let's talk about Love

By far and away the most important of these emotions is love, what one famous North American poet called "The only weapon of survival." So let's talk about love for a while.

The respected leadership coach Lance Secretan speaks to business leaders across North America. In his talks, his discussion often turns to the notion of love. If you want to see a group of confident, successful world leaders squirm, the word "love" will do the trick every time!

Emotion is not something that many business people wish to discuss. This is strange because emotion – investor fear, consumer confidence, shareholder trust, team-building camaraderie – is a huge part of what makes the business world go round. But love? Surely that has no place in the language of the business of giving?

Nothing could be further from the truth. In fact, love can be called "the glue that binds the giving process together." Whether it is love for family, for friends, for a community or neighbourhood, for a geographic place, or even for a memory, it is an emotion that triggers powerful response. One of these is the desire to give money in support of what is meaningful for the donor.

For most, it is appealing to feel connected to a community or neighborhood. Many of us have a very special place in our hearts for a little piece of the earth that we think of as uniquely ours. "Home is where the heart is," as the old saying goes.

To extend this further, people like the idea of good overcoming evil. Most feel a strong emotion for someone who triumphs against adversity. The concept of peace winning out over pain resonates exceptionally well. We love the idea of romance blossoming in unlikely places. Millions around the world of religious faith, take the word "love" to a very different place in their love of a higher power or being.

Love, in short, is the great connector – an emotion that in one way or another we experience many times a day in many different circumstances. Love tends to bring out our very best self. We accept the notion that giving is better than receiving or that personal sacrifice is worth it if someone else benefits.

So, if you truly wish to appear "worthy by default" in the eyes of your giving audience, your messages need to connect to them with love. Love drives all other emotions before it. If your message in some way cannot tug the heartstrings, it will have significantly less chance of success. The message "Every child deserves a bright future," is a very strong message. It appeals to our natural love of children, our connection to them, and the emotions that bind us to those who are smaller and less powerful than ourselves. It encourages us to give so that every child will, indeed, get the bright future that they deserve.

Consider these messages:

- Cancer can be beaten

- Help is just a phone call away

- Everyone knows someone who is touched by the United Way

- Save the Children

- Save the Whales

- Give the Gift of Life

All of these draw, either directly or obliquely, on the emotion of love. And all of them are exceptionally successful.

"Love is all you need," wrote John Lennon and Paul McCartney. When it comes to raising money, love may not be the whole answer – but it's a BIG part of it!

Two final things about being worthy by default

Number One: Never take your worthiness for granted. We only have to look at the sad history of child abuse and molestation in the Catholic Church to recognize that the "emotion by association" of religious belief and faith will not necessarily overcome the feelings of anger and disgust that unworthy behaviour immediately generates among worshippers and donors. Having said this, it is also true that the criminal acts of a few priests can be explained and, as with any group that is part of the general population of a community – whether it is a group of teachers, a group of athletes or a group of doctors – can be expected. But the reaction by those in authority in the Church – their attempts to cover up the crimes, their refusal to bring the individuals to justice once they were informed of their activities, their placement of these individuals into other positions where they might be able to abuse children again – created a feeling of anger and betrayal amongst believers.

One major reason why donations to the Catholic Church have slumped so badly in recent years is almost certainly because the organization has taken its worthiness for granted and has significantly damaged its relationships with the faithful and the generous.

Number Two: Never assume that others share your notion of worthiness, just because they "ought to." The Executive Director of a Children's Aid Society had very strong professional links to a small foundation whose sole purpose was to raise money for the society. Yet the Executive Director never gave the foundation any money himself.

When the foundation learned this, it was horrified. But the reason was simple. Even though the foundation had close links to his own organization, the Executive Director never personally felt that it was worthy. He had a strong concern about the salaries being paid to foundation staff. He felt they were exceptionally high in comparison to salaries at his own organization. For this reason, he could not bring himself to give. The foundation, at its core, was not worthy in his eyes.

Similarly, a board member on a fairly large humane society always made an annual donation and could be counted on to ask others for money. The society thought of him as a very strong supporter and loyal friend. That is, until they learned that he had recently made a six-figure donation to a humane society in a neighboring town; a far larger amount that he had ever contributed to his own organization.

The humane society was both angered and horrified. How could this be? But once again, the reason was relatively simple. The neighboring humane society practiced a very different form of animal euthanasia – one that the board member had been urging his own organization to adopt for many years, without success. In the donor's eyes, this made them more worthy of genuine financial support; and while he was still happy to donate time and money to his home society, when it came to the crunch, his big dollars went elsewhere.

CHAPTER 7:
BUILDING BRAND "WORTHY"

Another cornerstone of worthiness involves both building and standing by your brand.

More has been written about branding than any other element of marketing, selling and promotion – all of which are essential to help your organization survive and grow in the marketplace. The eternal question has always been "What is a brand?" This is rapidly followed by a second question: "How do you create and promote that brand?"

The best answer to the first question is probably this definition:

A brand is a collection of perceptions in the mind of the consumer.

Why is this a very good definition? First, because it is simple and easy to remember. Second, it reminds us that the brand is intangible and based on many value judgments made in the minds of many consumers. Thus, it is quite separate from any product or service that you may produce.

It is often argued that many organizations do not necessarily control their brands. Consumers do. Your brand exists in the mind of the consumer, who will ultimately determine its effectiveness.

Similarly, it is these customers who will build, strengthen and grow your brand by supporting you and working for you in the marketplace. Demand strengthens brand. So, your job is to stimulate demand by persuading consumers that your brand is valuable and one that is worthy of their support.

Take action to build your brand

So while the consumer may actually control the perception of the brand, you can take many significant actions to steer them towards a positive perception. This may ultimately mean that they give you the time and the dollars to help you achieve your aims.

Ten Ways to Build the Brand

1. Create a Unique Point of Difference (UPD) – what sets you apart.

2. Use the UPD in all marketing and promotional materials and initiatives.

3. Work out what your story is: and explain it in 75 words or less.

4. Ensure that everyone can articulate the story consistently.

5. Develop a professional logo and a consistent typographic style.

6. Use and enforce guidelines for their use and application.

7. Get professional help with your website and update it regularly.

8. Decide on your core target markets and aim all marketing at them; don't try to be all things to all people.

9. Use plain language, contemporary design and active writing for everything.

10. Do a few things consistently and well. Maintain focus and clarity.

Important considerations and actions in understanding your brand and making it clearly understood:

1. **Decide what your brand attributes are.** Attributes are the core strengths of your organization that you want the brand to represent. In business these might be items such as "most dependable," "stands behind product," "lowest price," "best overall value" and so on. One of the most useful attributes for a business brand is that the company stands behind its product or service with excellent warranties, guarantees and other forms of guaranteed customer satisfaction.

   For a charitable organization, brand attributes might be "passionate about our task," "low per capita cost for each dollar raised," "knowledgeable," "excellent people associated with us" and "honesty and transparency in all our dealings ".

   Whatever these attributes are, they need to resonate with the target audience. Consumers like to be directly associated with a brand – so that it becomes "their" brand. So your attributes must reflect the realities of the marketplace in which you do business, and the core values that make your organization stand out. They also need to mirror what donors and volunteers probably feel is most important to them.

   So first, determine your attributes. Do not make this a lengthy list.

2. **Be clear about what they mean.** Like your value statements noted earlier, it is important to understand clearly what your attributes mean.

   For example, what does the "Honesty and transparency" attribute mean? Does it mean that all of your financial statements and documents are open to everyone, regardless of why they may require them? Or does it mean that you consistently do the right thing, no matter what?

One small healthcare foundation once made a promise to one of its partner organizations that it would contribute $20,000 toward the cost of that charity's camp program. This promise was made months before the healthcare charity ran into considerable fundraising difficulties, primarily caused by the unexpected death of its leading fundraiser.

Even though it was now almost impossible for the healthcare foundation to make good on its original promise, it nevertheless went ahead and donated $20,000. This depleted its own financial reserves and put the organization at risk.

When questioned about this, the healthcare foundation's Executive Director said, "We felt we had no choice. We had made a promise, and the partner charity was counting on us. To break our promise would have been grossly inappropriate. We made the donation because we had a moral obligation to do so."

That is integrity. That is living up to you're the brand attributes that in this case were important to the organization.

Similarly, a charity devoted to providing children's gift packages at Christmas, listed one of its attributes as "hard work." At the height of its busiest season – early December – four of its delivery personnel who were responsible for making sure that children got their gifts in time, became seriously ill with the flu. It was obvious they would not be able to drive for three or four days.

Without hesitation, the Chair of the Board and three board members, all over 65 years old, worked tirelessly to find other delivery drivers, coordinate schedules, and ensured that packages were delivered on time so that there were no delays experienced by children and families anxiously waiting for their Christmas gifts. When others marvelled at this tremendous effort, the Chair of the Board simply shrugged and said, "Hard work means hard work. This is what we signed up for."

Mary Modahl, former vice president of marketing at Forrester Research in Cambridge, Massachusetts, and author of the book *Now or Never,* wrote:

"When you think of the brands that we all know, they mean something to us, and this is because they hold a promise. It is through the experience you have of the brands that the brand becomes true and the promise becomes real."

So, keep your promises! Back up your attributes with action.

3. **Be consistent.** Once you have worked out your brand attributes, you also need to deliver them consistently. Nothing breaks a brand faster than a failure to live up to attributes ALL THE TIME. For example, if one of your attributes is that you recognize and reward all donors appropriately, and you fail to send out a letter of thanks, a receipt or some other form of recognition, it is unlikely that the broken promise can be mended quickly. The donor suffers, and so does the brand.

   One cardiac care hospital listed a brand attribute as "The patient at the centre." On the surface, this seems like a "motherhood" statement. After all, if the patient is not at the centre of everything in a hospital, then who is?

   But in a survey recently conducted for the hospital, more than 96% of all patients said that they had experienced such an extraordinary level of consistent service from the hospital that the whole process of cardiac rehabilitation had become almost spiritual in nature.

   The survey showed that every single individual connected with the hospital – from the volunteer who first received patients at the door to the discharge nurse that finally sent them on their way after surgery – consistently practiced an extraordinarily high level of concern for patients. They treated each one of them as unique individuals, ensured that each one was given all the time they needed for questions and managed every little detail of care with precision, that patients actually said they felt "blessed" to have been part of that hospital experience. Now that is being consistent about your brand attributes!

4. **Understand what brand equity means.** Brand equity is another term for brand value. Essentially, it means the benefits that a good brand name and promise can contribute to your overall performance, strength and growth. This equity or value is influenced by a number of factors: the loyalty of volunteers and donors to your cause, general awareness and knowledge of your brand, your image and your regular, consistent performance. Brand equity is also influenced by the reputation and goodwill of people who work with you, your financial strength and your ability to deliver financial support.

In the charitable sector, just as in business, your brand value or equity can translate into significant dollars. If you have a strong brand, donors likely will be more attracted to you, and will tend to give you more money than if you are less well known or of questionable reputation. But the key is to reinforce that brand equity within the constituency that the organization serves directly.

Building Brand Value: Six Things to Think About

When building a brand, it is important to remember excellent advice given by Jim Collins in his book *From Good to Great*. The author reminds us that there are two ways to create brand value: the "flywheel" and the "loop of doom." You should put these in the order you are going to talk about them.

The flywheel approach recognizes that building a great brand is like pushing a flywheel around its circuit. You tend to push it slowly, one notch at a time, and in doing so carefully build strategies and actions that will hold up for a long period and demonstrate the true stability and quality of your brand.

The loop of doom, on the other hand, is a quick, short-term fix, designed to overcome what are often deep-seated challenges in an organization. Its aim is to put a band-aid over those long-term problems and hope that the brand or company will recover. As Collins points out, this very seldom happens. Instead, organizations that practice this technique usually spiral into a vortex of poor planning and thinking – the loop of doom – that ultimately destroys the brand and the organization completely.

The lesson here is clear: brand building takes time and is not a quick fix. Bearing that in mind, ask yourself the following questions:

1. **What is our core purpose?** What do we exist to do? Does everyone know our purpose and reason for being – our **Destiny Proposition?**

2. **What business are we really in?** Many charitable organizations forget that their core business is usually fundraising. Whether the recipients are churches, hospitals, colleges, environmental causes or sports organizations, funds still need to be raised to support them. It is very easy, for example, to forget that because you raise money for seniors, you are not in the gerontology business. You are still in the fundraising business. So be clear about what you really do and how you do it.

3. **How do we do what we do?** It is important to understand how you operate functionally in order to achieve your end results. For example, if most of your fundraising takes place through third-party events (where other people raise the funds and you are the recipient), then building relationships with third-party organizers is actually how you do what you do.

   Similarly, if most of your funds are generated by individual asks to major donors, you are in the solicitation business and need the core skills required to do that effectively. Another way to ask this question is "How do we get things done?" Focus on the core skills required to help you get results and keep that focus constantly.

4. **What are our goals?** Do they follow the very effective SMART formula: specific, measurable, achievable with effort, realistic and timely? Does everyone know what the goals are and how we plan to accomplish them?

5. **What messages define us?** This is not just the mission statement, nor is it the theme or branding statement, although both of these are important. Key messages are the simple, concise explanation of what we do and why we do it. Are we certain that everyone who works with us knows those key messages and can articulate them clearly?

6. **What key skills do we need?** These should be clearly defined and used whenever staff or volunteers are hired. As noted earlier, picking people to join your organization just because they say they are interested is not enough to ensure that you build the core skills you require.

When you can answer these questions, and know that all those who work with you can define them too, then you can focus on strengthening and building the brand. Here are five good ways to start.

Five Ways to keep the Brand Alive

1. **Do a few things consistently and well.** For example, be rigorous about how you select your board members and volunteers, as noted earlier. Or focus your communications on a first-class website and newsletter, and avoid the temptation to be visible with too many mixed messages in too many areas.

2. **Understand clearly what "quality" mean**s in your organization and practice it all the time. You may set standards, for example in how quickly donations are recognized. Your thank you letters may be true works of art. Your financial statements are above reproach. The best organizations always have a "quality statement" that identifies what they believe to be their top quality priorities. Then they integrate that statement into everything they say and do in support of the organization.

3. **Practice effective "positioning."** This means you need to have a clear idea of where your organization fits in the charitable spectrum in your community. You need a niche, a unique point of difference that sets you apart from all other charities that may be raising money for more or less the same things as you are. Defining that "position" is often challenging, but absolutely essential if you're going to build loyalty, a strong donor base, and messaging and promotion that tells your story effectively.

4. **Do the internal marketing first.** If your own people do not know what your brand stands for and how to communicate that effectively, no one else ever will. So start by making sure that your staff, board members, volunteers and all others associated with you know what it means to be "brand ambassadors."

5. **Evaluate your brand constantly.** The best organizations seek feedback and evaluation from their stakeholders whenever they can. Volunteer and donor satisfaction surveys, focus groups, performance reviews, and all the other standards tools of business should most certainly be applied if you want to have a truly fine brand that is responsive to the marketplace.

Ten Ways To Become Worthy

1. **Have a Destiny Proposition**, a clear sense of how you will positively change your world.

2. **Translate your Destiny Proposition into values** that underscore everything you do.

3. **Make sure that everyone understands** and lives those values.

4. **Make the right moral decision**s even if they cause you short- or long-term pain.

5. **Keep your promises.**

6. **Do a few things consistently well** and develop a reputation for them.

7. **Surround your organization** with people of probity, decency and good judgment.

8. **Be totally transparent**, even when you don't have to be.

9. **Know, protect and promote your brand**.

10. **Be a leader and advance the organization** toward making the world a better place.

PART II

CHAPTER 8:

SO, YOU ARE WORTHY.

NOW BECOME PREPARED

To steal and paraphrase a famous line from the movie *Field of Dreams*, "If you build it, they will come." We'd like to add "…so you'd better be ready."

In this film an Iowa farmer hears a voice as he works in his cornfield. The voice says, "If you build it, he will come." The "it" is a baseball diamond in his front yard. The "he" is one of a group of ghosts of long-dead baseball stars that magically arrives to use the diamond to play pick-up baseball.

When the farmer, played by Kevin Costner, was building "it" he didn't know who "they" were going to be. When the ghosts arrived, the farmer and his family didn't know what to think or do. What was the meaning of all this? How could they become prepared? What should they do next?

In the movie, everything is resolved. But the way an organization operates in its community is not tightly scripted and managed. Stuff happens – both good and bad. It is up to the organization to be ready for "it" - no matter what the situation. In this way, it can be ready for when the donor comes along. For most donors that make larger gifts, how prepared an organization is becomes a key factor in their decision-making.

Smaller organizations often ask why other, much larger charities seem to get the larger donations. They argue that their cause is just as compelling and just as worthy. That may be true. But the reality is that how well an organization is prepared for "It" has a direct bearing on donor confidence. When "he" comes, the donor needs to know unequivocally that the funds will be used correctly and efficiently.

This makes a huge difference to the ability to attract big gifts. If an organization does not have the capability to deal with larger gifts – if they aren't prepared – they can often mismanage the funds donated and, in some rare cases, the gift can put the organization out of business.

Here's example of how a large gift can actually take an organization to the brink of collapse. Some years ago a small organization opened in a mainly rural community. The group had a good group of dedicated volunteers that sat as Board members, worked as volunteer office staff and volunteers in the field. They got some grants from a government department to cover costs. Then they started to fundraise. Through events and direct solicitations they began to raise a little money to help them with their mission. In a good year they would raise perhaps $100,000. It was a welcome amount to enable a modest expansion of programs.

The Board, volunteers and the part-time staff were a happy group and felt that they were making a difference in their community and their world.

Then, out of the blue, someone gave them two million dollars.

A few months later, the charity was almost out of business. The staff, and most of the Board, quit. Volunteers walked away. Services were cut back. Funds dried up.

This meltdown was caused entirely by The Big Gift. The organization was not prepared for a gift of that size. But why? Why did a gift that all smaller organizations can only dream of cause this particular organization to melt down?

Large gifts normally come with large expectations. And to manage large expectations, the organization needs to be prepared. This does not mean that it has a bank account to receive the funds and knows how to write a receipt. That isn't being prepared. Being prepared, means first and foremost, that you understand the critical obligation you have to those who support you. They may be volunteers, donors, those who use your service and programs or government bodies that provide funding and in some cases, the authority that allows you to run your enterprise.

From that obligation must come a series of well thought-out policies, procedures and objectives that are constantly demonstrated and followed. This provides an operational discipline that instills confidence. It also gives those who are in charge the tools they need to deal with any situation: even a truly remarkable gift of support from an unexpected source.

The organization in our example was not prepared. When the large gift arrived, it could not even take a step back and ask itself, "Is this gift something we want?" How many organizations, even large ones, stop for a moment to ask that question? The answer is, very few.

If they had taken that step back, the Board and staff would have been able to focus on some fundamental issues. Can we use this gift provided to fund part of our long-term plan? If not, is the gift going to support something that we want to accomplish? If so, can we, in fact, accomplish it? Do we have the infrastructure to deal with it? Should we start and run a reserve fund with it? Could it be turned into an endowment? Is the donor someone we can work with as a partner?

All of these questions are a vital part of being prepared. If the money, great though it is, does not actually contribute positively to the organization and cannot be worked into a plan, is it wise to accept it?

The last question is particularly important because when the organization accepts a donation of this size, it also takes on a "partner." And partners, like their gifts, always come with some level of expectation that is generally larger and more specific then those that come with smaller annual donors. This is because they either have been asked to or expect to make a contribution that will change the fundamentals in some way – they will significantly help purchase a new piece of equipment or build a new building, or help advance research.

For larger organizations, partnerships are an accepted practice and structures are developed to make them happen. For smaller organizations, partnership is more difficult to carry out. Partners require time, understanding and in the end, commitment from the organization. When all three of these needs are not met, you have the potential for an angry or upset partner.

At the charity with the $2 million windfall, the donor had large expectations with good intentions of what the gift could achieve. But time and again, the organization disappointed the donor, because of its lack of preparation. The donor came rapidly to the conclusion that the organization was inept. It seemed unable to plan for the effective use of funds, had no clear process for developing new programs and, above all, could not help the donor realize his vision for the gift. In short, the organization was not prepared.

Many prominent philanthropists reinforce this point: if a donor's first reaction is that the organization is unprepared for a significant gift, a lot of hard work will be needed to get beyond this perception. The goal is always to build friendships and cultivate them so that friends become donors and donors become – if they are able – supporters in a transformational way. This is a common message when discussing major gifts. Connect. Cultivate. Ask. And then – Be Prepared.

So, if you build it, they will come and you had better be ready.

It all starts with the Prepared Matrix

Once organizations have figured out The Destiny Proposition –the statement of how they will make the world a better place – they then need to build The Prepared Matrix.

The Prepared Matrix is the development of essential OPERATING processes that make the Destiny Proposition a reality, that create a functional infrastructure and nurture strong partnerships.

While it is your Destiny Proposition and Worthiness that will attract donors to your cause, your potential partners still need and want to see facts, figures, plans, research and best practices before putting money on the table.

Just as business partners want to ensure that their funds will advance the business plan and make the company more profitable, donors want to be certain that their gifts will move the organization closer to its destiny. They will ask questions, raise expectations and expect tangible results. Are you ready?

Every organization, whether it recognizes it or not, creates a way of doing business that not only guides and leads the internal stakeholders – Board, staff and volunteers – but also sends a powerful message to all external stakeholders about what the organization truly believes.

Stakeholders receive these messages constantly, whether they are searching for them or not. Like people, charities are measured more by actions than by words, and their operating actions need to ring true with every audience.

Donors and potential donors are critical members of that audience. The larger the potential donation, the more the donor pays attention to, and analyzes the core operational processes and standards – the core belief – that is represented by the Prepared Matrix.

Some of these standards can be and are imposed upon the organization by outside bodies such as the IRS or Canada Revenue Agency. To keep a charitable registration number or charitable status – without which it is virtually impossible for the organization to raise funds through donations – basic benchmarks must be met.

Most organizations take the necessary steps without hesitation. But who sets the operating standards? Who determines the benchmarks for performance? What should the standards look like? How does the quality of operations affect the ability of the organization to truly make a difference and create a better world? Do those standards meet the needs of the increasingly interested donor as they make the decision whether or not to give a significant gift of support?

Only organizations with a Prepared Matrix, or perceived to have a Prepared Matrix, can truly benefit from transformational gifts of the kind that we see in newspapers and that are the envy of the sector!

An example of this is a foundation in a smaller community outside of Toronto. Charged with raising a certain target amount through major gifts each year by its founding Board, the Executive Director immediately created an organization that partnered with the right people and developed a Prepared Matrix.

By targeting individuals with a high name recognition factor to sit on the Board, the organization immediately created the perception that it knew what it was doing and gave itself instant credibility.

Next, the E.D. put into place a standard of operations that met or exceeded those that would normally be associated with a charity of this size. The organization quickly gained a number of significant gifts and rapidly came to prominence in its community, even in the face of significant competition from other charities that were vying for the same major gifts.

The Five Parts of the Matrix

Here are five elements of The Prepared Matrix, all of which are required if you are prepared and able to meet a donor's expectations. They will be covered in detail in the following chapters.

1. Get great financial protocols in place

2. Do an audit

3. Build a strong back office

4. Practice effective marketing

5. Use consultants wisely

The bottom line: You cannot just assume that there is a core group of people with the means and the will to give you large gifts that will unconditionally share your vision and just hand over the cash. One of the conditions for giving is that WHATEVER THE DONOR WANTS FROM THE GIFT can be achieved. You have to ensure that you can meet this fundamental, and vital, expectation.

Most fundraisers are essentially marketing people. They are not administrators, although many become excellent administrators and leaders. Their goal is to raise money. Many do so in organizations whose primary focus is not fundraising (i.e., universities, hospitals, etc.) where professional administrators and government regulations ensure that the operations of the organization, if not of the highest quality, at least have a tangible measuring stick by which to be judged. Donors can relate to these indicators easily and usually assume that they are in place.

Smaller organizations may be just as exceptionally well-run and efficient, but unless this is demonstrable, written down, codified and articulated, it will always be a tough story to tell to potentially large donors.

Let's go back to the example of the $2 million gift. The donor designated the gift toward the building of a new facility that the organization originally had no plans to build. Only when the funds were accepted was the decision made to move ahead. But a project of this size proved to be totally beyond the core competencies of the people involved. It was beyond their Prepared Matrix. The organization was unprepared and thus unable to deal with the desired outcome of the gift.

At first, there was an attempt to retroactively put the needed capacity into place. The organization's limited amount of available time, energy and organizational skill were focused almost completely on the new major donor's interest. But this had a consequence. Regular fundraising efforts dried up. Current programs began to stall. Those that would have been normally helped by the organization found their attentions diverted. Volunteers left. On the new initiative side, progress was so slow that the donor lost patience and discussed withdrawing the gift. By then, there were insufficient funds to carry on regular daily activities. The organization nearly collapsed.

What should have been a dream instead became a nightmare, one that could have been prevented if the small charity had been Truly Prepared.

CHAPTER 9:

BUILDING THE MATRIX — FINANCIAL PROTOCOL

Many smaller organizations simply fail at the process of financial monitoring. This is because most people, and by extension, most Board members do not understand financial process, reporting or accounting. In fact, when the discussion of accounting begins, their eyes glaze over.

One Board Treasurer who we know learned this the hard way when he made his reports. He put time and effort into the overall financial structures of the organization and at times, when things were good, many of his efforts were reported to a group whose attention was somewhere else.

This might have been all right. But when finances were not as good, the Treasurer could count on little or no comment or support for his ideas. A "head in the sand" mentality prevailed. Other than the Treasurer, no one could see the icebergs ahead. When they hit, the organization was unprepared. Clearly, this was not a healthy situation.

Typically organizations rely on volunteer financial professionals or accountants to handle the financial aspects of the Board's mandate. They depend on their knowledge, trust them to do the right thing and, in the end, hope for the best.

This is a clear abrogation of responsibility. Every Board and staff member should have a working knowledge of finances, be able to articulate the financial position of the organization, know how funds are raised and distributed and be able to read the budget. If they do not know how, they should be taught. Generous donors expect fiscal probity from everyone, not just the experts.

In particular, processes should focus on: receipt of and processing of donations, daily bookkeeping (including regular banking) and budget creation and regular reporting. There should also be ironclad systems in place for receiving, receipting, recording and recognizing donations.

An additional consideration is dealing with organizational investment, including the receipt of stocks and bonds as donations. Finally, the organization must understand how and why an audit of financial statements is conducted and engage in this on a yearly basis (this is mandatory, but many very small organizations often feel that the expense is too great and don't bother).

This is not a book about detailed accounting and bookkeeping procedures and standards. There are many fine books and other resources on this topic, all of which are excellent resources for any organization that wishes to establish complete financial management policies and procedures. But it is important that we provide an overview of some of the basics of these important undertakings. Donors need to know and trust that these practices are in place. They will want proof that you are dealing with these issues proactively and in a disciplined manner.

This sounds like overkill to many smaller organizations. Groups with moderate yearly revenue may baulk at the required work. But creating a disciplined "best practices" approach is imperative. If you don't have a way of tracking and reporting on your funds, in the most rigorous way possible, donors will not give. "Trust us" doesn't work. "Show us" is what donors expect.

Four ways to ensure fiscal responsibility

First, hire a credible accountant who will do your audit and help you oversee the work of your volunteers. Negotiate the best possible rate based on the firm's notion of community service. Tender the contract every two or three years. Ideally, find a firm that is highly respected in the community. Their "street cred" will rub off on you.

Next, create an annual report – nothing extravagant is necessary – and send it to selected donors and stakeholders with a covering letter from the Chair of the Board. Make your finances public. This is always a tricky notion because many groups feel that they are not efficient enough or impressive enough to register in the minds of donors. Publicity, they feel, is a negative. In reality, what this signals to the community is that the organization has

94 – WORTHY AND PREPARED

nothing to hide and is proud and willing to promote its sound financial management process.

Third, seek out advice from community leaders who can provide important input into the way the finances are managed. Connecting with local professionals to get their opinion allows them do some volunteer work without taking on too large a burden of time and energy. It also signals to the community that your commitment to financial management is serious and that your efforts will go beyond the standard levels of due diligence.

Fourth, practice very strong bookkeeping. This in one area where you cannot afford to cut corners. If you do not have in-house or volunteer capacity to run a set of books that will stand up to the most rigorous tax or charitable status audit, you need to invest in this service immediately. And you need strong financial protocols in place, as noted.

CHAPTER 10:
CONDUCTING AN ORGANIZATIONAL AUDIT

Before you get directions to any destination, you need to know where you are starting from to learn how to get where you are going. This is as true for small charities as for anyone else.

The best way to know where your organization is right now is to conduct an audit of your operations.

The audit may be function-specific (financial practices or marketing, for example), and the results and conclusions will be as different as the organizations that conduct them. The desired outcomes are improvement and change. A good audit, which usually involves input from many stakeholders, will always suggest constructive ways to improve and provide steps required to achieve progress.

The willingness to review, propose and engage change helps you in two ways. It focuses the organization as it moves toward its destiny. It is also a wonderful way to engage others, as it demonstrates that you are willing and capable of soliciting and accepting input.

Many organizations do not want to have their processes reviewed or questioned. Change is tough. Admitting that you need to change is even tougher. Ways of doing things become entrenched, practices become habitual. Seeking out and adopting best practices from elsewhere can be time-consuming and hard work.

But – and it's a big but – any small charity that is unwilling to seek and accept outside input and cannot take transform that input into the very core of how it operates is unlikely to grow and succeed. It is generally those that are willing to engage in a regular review of their process, at every level, that are truly successful.

Larger institutions with more constituents are regularly examined by both internal and external forces. This helps to create a climate of constant re-evaluation. While the scrutiny can be exhausting, it does force the organizations to examine their "best practices" that stakeholders and others expect them to adopt.

But most charities are small. They have budgets and staffs that in the business world may be equivalent to a tiny family-run or private venture. These smaller not-for-profits DO have a full complement of volunteer Directors with great passion for the cause. They routinely question, monitor and govern all aspects of the charity, opening themselves to tremendous public scrutiny. That scrutiny focuses the work of the professional staff. At every turn, their assumptions are questioned and feedback is constant.

So it should be a small step for a small charity to extend that scrutiny further and carry out an audit. This review is one of the best ways to provide proper insight into the workings of the organization, and to demonstrate to others that you are fully prepared.

An organization that focused on addiction therapy had for years relied on its administrative officer to handle the majority of their operational needs, leaving the professionals – trained social workers with expertise in addiction therapy – to deal with the actual services to the clients they served. It was the administrative officer that was the liaison with the board on financial matters, with the auditors at audit time and with vendors and suppliers.

Every month the administrative officer would provide the overview and answer the questions asked. This particular organization – like many smaller charitable groups – seemed to be in constant financial difficulty. Each time it was the administrative officer that would identify the problems, offer suggestions for correction and be given the power to carry out any action agreed to by the Board. In the end, a solution would be found and the officer was praised.

When the auditors came in to do their yearly audit, if problems were discovered or inconsistencies found, it would be the administrative officer that would provide the answers. This went on for 20 years. Even though the Board often wondered why there seemed to always be problems with the finances and why only the administrative officer understood the overall financial picture, no one ever called for an audit of the financial management policies or procedures. No one ever asked the auditors to do more.

When the administrative officer left for another job, the organization was quickly immersed in a new and more dangerous financial crisis that threatened the continued operation of the organization. In the end, the necessary audit and overview was undertaken, not by design but out of need. It was a need brought on by a crisis, rather than by process and good management and leadership.

When the audit was conducted it was found that nothing illegal or malicious had taken place. But the administrative officer had been allowed to operate in his own way for a long time. This created idiosyncratic processes and institutional knowledge that was located in the head of the administrative officer and not in the policies and procedures of the organization.

Some things to remember when doing the audit

You will benefit from having an independent contractor to do the audit itself – possibly on a pro bono basis or for a small honorarium. While you should definitely be prepared to put the whole process out to tender and engage a fully remunerated consultant, try the less expensive option first!

1. **Know what you want.**

    Understand what you are attempting to accomplish. This is not a review of your mission but of how the organization operates. It is also not a performance review for staff. An audit assesses operations. Is the marketing program doing its job? Do we have the right human resource protocols in place? How useful is our database, and are we using it correctly? Could we be more creative about raising money?

    The audit should also include a review of Board processes and governance models. One school of thought says that volunteer Board members should be held to a slightly lower standard of performance and diligence than if they were paid. Nothing could be further from the truth. A Board's main task, to be stewards of the enterprise, is a sacred trust. How it fulfills that trust can make or break your charity, so audit the Board just as you would the volunteer management program, or anything else.

Remember the philanthropists who look first at the composition and operation of the Board before they decide if they will give. In doing so, they make a clear statement that the Board matters. Any Board that decides not to review its own activities shows a clear lack of understanding of its own role and value in the giving process.

2. **Take ownership of the process.**

For an audit to be successful, it has to be championed. Board and staff must commit fully to the process and its results. They also need to make it clear that once the audit report is presented and accepted (assuming it is), then change, whether simple or transformational, will take place. Finally, they need to drive that change.

Those who disagree with the findings – whether Board or Staff – can voice that disagreement but must abide by the results. Disagreement often happens. Most healthy and functional Boards bring great differences of opinion to the table. Having a number of perspectives is positive. What isn't positive, but often occurs, is that Boards agree in a vote and then the nay sayers criticize the decision in public.

The Board must take full ownership of the audit, fully support it in public and do everything they can to make it happen. Otherwise, the process will be interesting, but in the end, useless. It will be business as usual. An audit is a confidence-builder for those that want to support you in a truly significant way. They want to see stability, leadership and trust and it is the organization's duty to provide it to them. No amount of good intentions or fine language will convince them otherwise, if the operational reality they see does not meet their expectations. You cannot simply say, "Trust us." They won't. If the organization is truly going to make the world a better place, it has to start by making itself a better organization. Actions speak!

3. Talk to internal stakeholders first.

The process should begin with candid information gathered from as many internal sources as possible. Try to ensure that the auditor speaks to individuals, not groups. People are more candid when approached on their own. There are many intelligent and thoughtful members of the organization that may not have the opportunity to provide their input on a regular basis. This is a great way to receive their insights and to deepen their own connection with the organization.

Don't make the mistake of only talking to people at the "top" of the organization. A saying in business suggests that "all real knowledge in the organization rests at the bottom," with the people who are closest to the customers and the marketplace. So take the time to speak with a novice volunteer as well as the 10-year veteran. Talk to the janitor and the receptionist just as respectfully as you would to the Board chair.

4. Next, talk to others.

The review must also include candid information gathered from as many external sources as possible. If this group of proves to be far too large to accommodate easily, select a representative sampling. They can add an outsider's perspective that will be fresh – and without any preconceived historical perspective or personal agenda. They will also ask the obvious questions that those too close to the organization may miss.

Engaging outside stakeholders brings them closer to the organization, gives you new ideas and insights and may encourage many of them to support you – either for the first time or more than before. People like to help, so engage them fully in the audit.

5. Then, talk to the people you serve.

The most important group in any audit is the end users, those who benefit from your support through services or funding. This sound obvious, but interestingly, this is a group that is often overlooked.

A group of service and government agencies recently came together with a funding program to help children to access sports program their families could not afford. The group consulted with many charitable groups and collaborated thoroughly with each other. They quickly developed processes to help families apply for and receive the necessary funds.

But at no time did the group ask some fundamental questions of the families themselves. For example: is our assessment of your financial situation too invasive? Is the application process easy enough? Is our information material useful?

Instead, assumptions were made: the best possible assumptions and ones that truly had the best interests at heart for recipients. They came from thoughtful professionals who were truly passionate about the work. But the families were not happy. Many found it difficult to locate information and to use the on-line application process. Others thought the financial data required was too comprehensive. Parts of the process did not make sense.

A few simple questions presented to a cross-section of users would have avoided many problems that later became apparent. But it didn't happen, and the process suffered as a result.

6. Talk to other organizations

One of the great things about the not-for-profit sector is the willingness of most groups to be generous and share information, advice and wisdom to colleagues in the sector. Of course, there are closely guarded secrets –

donor lists, long term plans, and so on. But aside from some obviously proprietary data, most are happy to discuss their best practices.

So, seek out these generous colleagues. Evaluate their success. Take what works and seems to fit, feel comfortable enough to discard what seems out of place. Even if you connect with only three to four organizations, you are bound to get some information that will help you to move forward and become even more prepared.

7. Make It Happen

Consider forming an independent Board committee to over see the audit process. Use this committee as a centre of influence and mine its community connections to give you access to any expertise you need. It should operate at arm's length from the Board; able to make its own decisions but still accountable to the Board for the final report.

This is often a wonderful way for busy professionals in a community to fulfill their desire to volunteer. They can do this with a short-term and finite project that may fit better with their schedules than taking on a full Board commitment. Often, other professionals from non-competing organizations may be available to assist in the process.

Also remember to include staff on the committee. Staff members of not-for-profits are passionate about what they do. And, they have thought about how to be successful in advancing the mission and services of the organization.

8. Report Properly

No matter how the exercise is carried out, a formal presentation of the findings must be made to the Board of Directors. This can take many forms, but it should begin by explaining the methodology used, followed by an overview of the process, timelines and a budget, and conclude with a summary of recommendations. If the review is carried out by a Board committee, that committee needs to take ownership of the recommendations.

Those receiving the review and its recommendations need to have an open mind and thick skin. The exercise is not one of criticism, but rather an attempt to build a better organization. If gaps and weaknesses are found and solutions are offered, then the group performing the task should be applauded, no matter what their opinions.

Board members unhappy with the conclusions should re-double their efforts to be cooperative and become engaged in the process to make the organization better.

One thing to avoid is to single out staff when faults are found. Audits can certainly provide a very real expression of difficulties within an organization. The quick response may be to blame staff and clean house. But staff must be given a chance to deal with the gaps and weaknesses discovered and should be supported fully in this effort.

9. Get it Done!

Now comes the hard part. Putting an audit into practice is easier said than done. New practices and approaches are often difficult to accept, even when an organization willingly undertakes the process of self-examination.

Sensitive change management is essential. Just because the new approach is well-researched, well-presented and well-accepted doesn't mean it won't be difficult to implement. There are some people who may have entrenched places in the organization or feel that specific programs are their personal areas of responsibility. These people may not conform to initiatives that place that "ownership" in jeopardy.

The NIMBY (Not In My Back Yard) principle often applies. In more organizations than we can count, Board and staff welcome ANY changes that do not apply to their special area of interest. They are equally adamant that anything they are personally involved with should stay the same. Or they look at the recommendations through a lens of self-interest and interpret the outcomes through that lens. Some people simply refuse to change the way they to do things.

This is when leadership is essential. Jerold Panas, the eminent fundraiser, talks about the passion of those who wish to advance the mission of the organization and how they embrace change. True visionaries understand that organization's history, while important, can be a barrier to long-term success. Instead of focusing on what has been done in the past, they should focus on what they can become. As Joel Barker said in his pivotal work on paradigms, "your past success guarantees you nothing in the future."

While it is true that one should not repeat the mistakes learned from history, it is also true that the organization must live in the moment…and plan for the future.

Race car drivers understand this fact. In the middle of a race, they do not think about how they navigated a really tough turn the last time. Rather, they fully focus on navigating the corner now. What happened before will not necessarily help them the next time. Far too often organizations allow the experiences of the past to define how they will act in the future. This can be a true handicap.

For example, consider the organization that runs a very extensive Christmas program that provided in-home gifts and food to seniors in need. Board members and volunteers with the program made most operational decisions each Christmas season based on the results and challenges of the previous year. Because the program ran intensely for only two months each year, they were blessed with plenty of time to consider all the ways the program could be made better.

But when they were approached with the possible merits of moving from a paper record-keeping system to an electronic one – creating a more streamlined and speedy process able to accommodate the ever-increasing demands on the program – they resisted. They had become accustomed to the manual and cumbersome "paper trail" that had been built up over years of service. So instead of looking at ways to make an obviously better way work effectively, they spent their time trying to refine an outdated process that had long since ceased to be useful – or easy to administer.

Each charity will be unique in the way it interprets and implements an audit. One key to success is a plan with a timeline. The timeline has to include realistic targets for certain parts of the program to be implemented and benchmarks, or progress points, to ensure that it is progressing well.

With these, you are not necessarily holding anyone's feet to the fire. Rather the organization is simply setting a plan to get from here to there. The desired outcome of any audit is to create an interconnected process of operations that ensure the organization is as well run as possible. It may seem like a complex process for a small charity, but it is crucial for the long-term advancement of the organization.

CHAPTER 11:
BUILDING THE MATRIX —
HOW GOOD IS YOUR BACK SHOP?

Business history is littered with tales of organizations that build a strong image, develop a great product and create sales, but completely ignore the development of good "back shop" services that support everything being done on the surface.

The shipping department cannot keep up with orders. Product complaints and concerns are routinely ignored. Promised delivery dates are missed. Very often, invoicing and receipting are sloppy and filled with errors.

One of Canada's best-known grocery chains recently struggled with inventory management and control. Staple items, such as cereals, canned goods or detergent products, were often not available, with no indication of when they might appear on the shelves. Not surprisingly, the reputation of the grocery chain slipped immediately. There were tales in the media of management struggles, disagreements over strategy and concerns that the chain might be bought out by a major U.S. competitor.

It took several years for the company to reorganize itself and ensure that its shelves were stocked. But in the meantime, its share price and market share dipped considerably, and significant damage was done to its reputation as an industry leader.

It is easy in the charitable sector to assume that such rigorous standards do not apply. In fact, the opposite is true. When you are handling and managing other people's money – regardless of whether you are a professional or volunteer-based agency – you need to be doubly rigorous to ensure that you meet the highest possible levels of performance. As we have seen, donors will only contribute toward an organization that they believe is truly worthy. Having a great back shop to handle their gifts in an appropriate manner is an essential part of worthiness.

Take a look of this story from one of North America's leading hospital foundations. Some years ago it decided to take an aggressive approach to its planned giving program.

Developing a planned giving program is a long-term proposition. Potential donors have to be contacted well in advance of that moment when their will or estate may come into play. This has to be done with tact and grace, and a long-term relationship has to be developed with the donor in order for a planned gift to be realized sometime in the future. Nothing can be allowed to jeopardize this relationship, particularly when it is being nurtured in the early stages.

In the hospital foundation's aggressive approach, it decided to enlist an outside agency to help it identify top potential donors of estate gifts. The hospital decided to engage a very sophisticated telemarketer to speak with each potential donor about planned gifts. Once this initial contact had been made, hospital staff would follow up on the information gathered from phone calls and create a file on each donor that could be used to build a relationship.

The phone campaign began without a hitch. In fact, it went so well that literally hundreds of potential donors indicated a willingness to participate with a planned gift. The hospital had done its work so well for so many years that donors immediately found it worthy of support and were prepared to commit significantly to it.

The hospital, while obviously pleased with this tremendous response, was caught flat-footed. It had neither the staff, nor the resources, to deal properly with the overwhelming response. Cracks immediately began to appear in the entire campaign.

Staff resigned under the pressure, information was not gathered, files fell into disrepair, and the proper follow-up was never achieved.

The hospital suspended the program. It only restarted it 12 months later, with a much less aggressive approach. The original donor prospects were either completely lost to the hospital or the careful process of cultivation had to begin anew.

The damage was done. Not only did the hospital's reputation for worthiness suffer, but the success of the phone solicitation was completely wasted and a major potential source of revenue was placed in jeopardy. Perhaps more significantly, internal morale declined and the necessary momentum for a successful planned giving program was lost.

Consider also the case of a small community foundation, based in a town of about 20,000 people. For many years this foundation had administered and invested funds for its donors. It had always been modest in its goals and objectives, being quite content to handle relatively small amounts of money and administer grants to equally small community groups and organizations.

All went well for many years, until one day the foundation unexpectedly received a major gift of stock and securities, as well as several large gifts-in-kind that could be re-sold by the charity to generate funds.

Initially, there was rejoicing. These gifts would immediately double the size of the foundation, extend its ability to offer grants to many more organizations, and enhance its reputation and image for worthiness.

But, there was a problem. The foundation had no previous experience in dealing with stocks and securities. The back shop did not know to handle them. The investment committee, accustomed to dealing with much smaller donations, did not know how to invest the money effectively, and arguments broke out.

Similarly, the board of directors was split on how to assess the value of the gifts-in-kind, how to determine an appropriate selling price, how to market them and whether or not to use some of the money to help build the foundation's staff and resources. Some members felt all the money should be used for charitable purposes, while others argued that the foundation needed to build its capacity to allow it to accept more gifts of this size by increasing staff and resources.

Rather like our earlier friends who resigned when confronted with a $2 million gift, the subsequent strain on the organization proved to be its undoing. Many of the board members resigned, and appropriate replace-ments could not easily be found.

The original donor, upset with the way in which his money was handled, withdrew some of the original gift, which meant that the foundation had to break some of its promises to potential recipients. In only a few short months after the major donation, the foundation wound itself down.

In the eyes of the donor, it had been worthy. But in real-world terms it had been not prepared.

The lesson is clear. If your back shop is not able to support your upfront efforts to attract donors, you will inevitably fail. Being prepared, in the best sense of the word, means having an effective back shop.

At a minimum, an organization that is fully prepared, needs the following fundamentals in place to create a strong back shop.

- **Provide prompt follow-up to telephone calls and e-mails.** How often have we heard someone say, "Leave me a message and I will get back to you within 24 hours," and then never hear a word? Similarly, in today's "hurry up" world, it is expected that all e-mails will at least be acknowl-edged promptly, if not replied to in full.

- **Ensure quick turnaround time on receipts and thank you letters.** We know of a donor who once gave a local charity $10,000, which was the biggest single gift he had ever made, and also represented a size-able donation for the organization. After two weeks, he had no official acknowledgment of the gift. After four weeks, the same thing. Finally, embarrassed, he asked the charity if the gift had arrived and was told that it had, although the staff member answering the call did not verbally thank the donor. The donor requested an official acknowledgement, but none came. Two more months passed. And then another two months. Finally, a full eight months after the original gift was sent, a receipt and thank you letter arrived. Needless to say, the donor has not given such a sum to the organization again and has told many other people about the experience.

- **Provide the donor with appropriate information.** Too many charities send out a standard package when asked for details of the operation. Instead, each package should be customized as much as possible to the needs and interests of the recipient.

How to create a prepared back shop

1. Ideally, a human voice that answers the phone and a real live receptionist at the door.

2. A voice mail system that is simple, easy to use and logical.

3. A private area where confidential meetings and interviews can be held.

4. An e-mail protocol that emphasizes good manners, good grammar and responsible messaging.

5. 24-hour turnaround on receipts and thank you letters.

6. Properly developed financial statements, open to public scrutiny.

7. An annual financial audit that is transparent.

8. Up-to-date technology to the extent that a budget will allow.

9. Proper recording of all gifts and adherence to all local tax laws about giving.

10. On-going training for staff as the budget will allow.

11. An effective volunteer recruitment, orientation and training program.

12. Ditto for the Board.

13. Recognition of all gifts, no matter how small.

14. Speed of response to any and all requests – for anything!

CHAPTER 12:
BUILDING THE MATRIX —
MAKE IT WITH MARKETING

Regis McKenna, the marketing whiz who showed Steven Jobs how to get his Apple computer out of the garage and into computer immortality, coined the famous phrase, "Marketing is everything and everything is marketing."

On the surface, this seems highly unlikely! Isn't fundraising everything? Or accounting? Or perhaps volunteer management? All of these things are essential for the effective operation of a charitable organization and surely marketing is only one of the components in which you need to be successful?

What McKenna means is that marketing drives many of the functions that really make a business or charity successful. It creates image and perception as we have seen. It builds goodwill for an organization, and for a charity, that translates quickly into dollars. It demonstrates success that attracts people to become part of that success. It tells stories that appeal to many audiences for many different purposes.

An anonymous guru once wrote, "Marketing is the oil that greases the wheel of progress." Used most effectively, marketing (and its sister disciplines of publicity and promotion) can create a climate of achievement and energy that attracts buyers, sellers, donors, volunteers: whoever an organization needs to grow, survive and prosper.

A quick Google search shows that there are tens of millions of links to marketing information. In fact, it has been said that only sex has a higher number of links on the web! For now, let's focus on ten "home truths" about marketing and promotion that you need to remember to get the results you need from the resources you have.

Home Truths

1. **Never assume that people know what you are doing.** One of the biggest mistakes we often make is to think that, because we are so actively involved with our charity and know so much about it, then this must be true of everyone else as well. In fact, we often discover that even those who are closest to our operation – for example, Board members – actually

know only a fraction of what we are all about. The assumption that our story is well known is probably the biggest mistake that we can make and as a result, we do not tell it either well or completely.

Try this very simple exercise: develop a brief True or False quiz of 25 questions about your charity. Give it to your Board members and closest volunteers to work on in teams. See how many of them can correctly answer more than 75% of the test. Chances are high that very few of them can do this. This little quiz will not only reinforce the importance of marketing, it may help you decide which areas you need to promote and discuss in order to build your stakeholder knowledge base.

2. **If you don't fill the vacuum of awareness, it will fill itself.** Many years ago, the manufacturers of a world famous soft drink did a study to see what would happen to their business if they stopped marketing and promoting the brand completely. The results showed that would likely go out of business in about three years. Why? Because once a vacuum of unawareness is created about any business – once information about it drops out of sight or out of mind – other things move in to fill the gap. In the case of the soft drink company, those "other things" would have been competitors' marketing messages. For us, it means that misinformation will probably move in to fill the gap. Or worse, it means that dollars and human resource support will flow to other organizations which may be equally worthy – but who support a very different cause from ours.

Marketing is all about filling the vacuum of unawareness and doing so on a regular basis. In a pivotal study in 1961, Robert Lavidge and Gary Steiner developed what was known as the "advertising awareness curve." This traced how many advertising messages were required to move a potential customer from a position of complete unawareness about an organization to a position where that customer became an active buyer.

The curve traced the progress of a customer through a series of steps, ranging at the bottom from a complete lack of knowledge about the business through to increased knowledge, awareness, liking, preference, trial and final purchase.

Even in the early 1960s, when advertising was not nearly as comprehensive and invasive as it is today, the study showed that it could take as many as 40 advertising impressions to move the customer through that series of steps. The lesson was very clear. If you want to truly make an impression with your target market, you have to keep marketing on a regular basis.

For charities with limited time and money, this presents a real challenge. But if good principles of marketing and promotion are followed, it is possible to maintain a consistent presence in your marketplace without spending a ton of cash.

3. **Remember the Rule of Seven.** A critical principle of good marketing is to remember this rule about people's ability to remember things. Another simple game demonstrates this rule very easily. Ask your Board members to take an index card and write down the top news stories of the day. We suggest you eliminate sports, as this is too easy! Focus instead on current affairs – national and international – that are highlighted in the media at the time. Give everyone about a minute to do this.

   Once they have completed this exercise, ask them to turn the card over. Get them to jot down as many brand names as they can remember of a typical household product: cereal, perhaps, or cookies. Then compare the results of the two cards.

   Chances are very good that on the news card, very few Board members will have managed to register more than seven items. On the flip side of the card, they will probably have done much better. This is because the human mind can generally only retain no more than seven items in its short-term memory for things that are relatively unfamiliar. The more commonplace the items are – such as cereal, for example – the easier it is for people to remember more. This is known as the Rule of Seven.

Keep this rule firmly in mind when developing your promotion and marketing materials. Not only should your message be relatively simple and straightforward, it should be built around only three or four key messages, statements or values – or whatever seems appropriate. And once you have developed these "key messages," keep on repeating and restating them at every opportunity.

Don't try to be like the famous metaphor of humorist Stephen Leacock and get on a horse so that you can gallop off in all directions. Far too many promotional materials try to do too much, tell too many stories and end up confusing the marketplace. Keep the messages clear, simple and concise – and, most important of all, keep repeating them! (We just repeated ourselves on that one!)

4. **Remember benefits and features.** All good promotional materials need to be written in a way that directly appeals to the audience. This sounds obvious, but is one of the most difficult things to do effectively, because it means clearly knowing the difference between "benefits" and "features."

A "benefit" is anything about your organization that helps or benefits the reader. A "feature" is how you deliver that benefit. Very often, the difference between the two is how you use the language.

Here's a simple example. Is this statement, "We have been in business 100 years" a benefit or a feature? In fact, it's a feature. The benefit of our longevity to the reader might be that we are stable, reliable, highly experienced and worthy of their business, because we have learned a great deal from being around all this time. The actual fact of being in business for 100 years is not a benefit in and of itself. It is how we deliver the benefits just noted that matters.

Another example: Is the statement, "We are open 24 hours a day" a benefit or a feature? Again, it's a feature. The benefits of this service are that we are always there when you need us, and we are totally convenient. How we got to be that way is because we are open 24 hours a day.

It is worth remembering this very simple tip. If most of your literature starts with the word "We" ("We have many funds for you to invest in" or "We help teenage moms to feel better about themselves," then chances are good that you are describing features.

Better options would be to say something like, "You get flexibility of choice from the wide range of our investment funds," or, "Teen moms receive life-affirming experiences because of your generosity".

Marketers often use a mantra that goes like this: "Lead with benefits, follow with features." Make your benefit statements the most compel-ling thing in your marketing materials, and then support them with the features that help you deliver those benefits. Confusing benefits and features or worse, ignoring benefits altogether to talk only about what "we" do, is one of the most fundamental marketing mistakes.

5. **Protect your image at all costs.** As we have seen, your image or brand is one of your most important weapons in the fight to gain charitable dollars. Ensure that everything you do reinforces and reflects the quality of that brand. Poorly-produced marketing materials – ones that do not follow fundamental principles of good promotion and publicity – will ultimately do you great harm. Using old, tired clip art or graphic tech-niques that were out-of-date more than a decade ago will create a very negative perception of your brand. Bad grammar, poor spelling, untidy syntax and passive writing will also reflect negatively.

Many charities believe that because they are run on a shoestring, they can "get away" with materials that look cheap and shoddy. Not so. In fact, such materials will probably guarantee that the charity remains small and poor for many years to come. People support organizations that they perceive to be highly professional, well-run and able to tell their story in a contemporary and effective way.

6. **Do a few things very well.** Build your entire marketing and promotional campaign around no more than three or four initiatives – and focus on doing these as well as you can. These might include: a) a very effective web site; b) a well-produced and printed case statement; c) an information folder or brochure that highlights your mission, mandate and programs; d) some small teaser advertisements that draw people to your website so that they can learn more about you; e) two or three very well-written speeches or presentations, with slides, that can be used at speaking engagements and conferences; f) possibly a FaceBook or Twitter page or Huddle chat room where volunteers can share ideas and perspectives with each other.

Obviously, what you decide to do will be based on your own unique needs and the marketplace in which you work. But it will always be better to focus your time, resources and talents on doing "more with less."

7. **Take advantage of technology.** There is really no excuse for not using technology to its fullest in order to tell your story. One key principle today is to make your website the focal point of all your marketing and promotion efforts. Once designed, it is very inexpensive to administer and run, can be changed daily, is highly interactive with your target markets, and can carry far more information attractively and appealingly than any print material or other marketing initiative can manage. Using Google analytics or a similar tool, you can track all "hits" and traffic on your site, and gain a highly accurate picture of its effectiveness.

Obviously, you don't want to disenfranchise those people who may still not be "web savvy." But this group is declining rapidly every day. Be sure to highlight your website in all your other materials. For example, instead of placing large, expensive print advertisements develop small, eye-catching ones that grab the reader's attention with an interesting fact and also provide the website address.

An added advantage of moving most of your marketing to the web is that you can significantly reduce traditional print costs and use the money you save for funds to support your giving commitments or other operating costs.

While the "jury is still out" on whether tools such as Twitter and FaceBook can be used effectively by charities, they are rapidly gaining popularity of all around the world, and cannot be ignored as social marketing tools to help you build energy, excitement and interest in your charity. You can also develop highly effective e-newsletters at a fraction of the cost of printed ones, eliminate the mailing costs and use software effectively to personalize each issue and also track "who reads what."

8. **Don't forget face-to-face communications.** No matter how effective technology is, nothing beats the power of face-to-face marketing. Speaking engagements, panel discussions, small group meetings, focus groups, personal presentations – anywhere where real people can talk about your charity – are extremely powerful.

   If you have board members or volunteers who are already capable presenters, take full advantage of them. Service clubs, professional associations, Church groups, Chambers of Commerce and many other community ventures are always eager for speakers. Use some of your resources to develop a strong, interactive presentation and get in front of people as much as possible. Again, make sure your messages are simple and consistent. And also ensure that your speakers can successfully handle any potential question that may come along. Presentations often rise or fall on the success of the speaker's ability to answer questions, so make sure you can anticipate and deal with any potential question that arises from face-to-face encounters.

9. **Recognize when you need professional help.** Almost everybody thinks they are expert in marketing, because they can read, write, listen and practice all forms of human communication. But marketing is a highly-

developed skill and cannot always be left up to amateurs. If you already have talented marketers in your organization, then by all means seek out their skills and knowledge. If not, don't hesitate to call in professional help if you need it.

Because your logo and image are so important, professional assistance in this area is essential. You may also decide to get advice to develop your key messages and how to articulate them. Similarly, professionals can help you decide how to spend your limited dollars most effectively. Do not entrust the design of your website to the tech-savvy teenager who may be a keyboard wizard, but cannot be expected to have the maturity, insight and passion that is required to build this cornerstone of your marketing campaign. It is easy to be "penny wise and pound foolish" when it comes to professional help. Think of the cost as a long-term investment in your survival and growth.

10. **Finally, never stand still.** Refresh and update your promotional materials constantly. The old saying that "familiarity breeds contempt" is very true when it comes to publicity and promotion. Think how often you have cursed when you see a TV advertisement for the 500th time. Your instant reactions are frustration, boredom and anger that you are still being bombarded with something so old and tired. Don't assume that your marketplace will forgive stale and outdated messages. This is particularly true of your website, of course, but also applies to everything else you do.

Of course, ultimately marketing will only be successful if it contributes to the achievement of your goals. Measuring the true impact of marketing has always been difficult; but consider the alternative.

Without a strong marketing, promotion and publicity program, your organization has the same result as you when you wink at someone else in the dark. The only one who knows what you are doing is you! Tell your story proudly, and grow strong!

Marketing and Relationship-building

While you obviously cannot connect with every community group and organization in your market, you do need to reach out to those who can help build your brand, tell your story, connect you to donors and enhance your image.

This is especially true for small charities that may not have high-profile board members, big marketing budgets or high-impact programs and services. Larger organizations, such as hospitals, can often reach out to the community by the sheer size and scope of their operations.

Others, such as humane societies, may be able to connect because of their very unique niche. Still others may be able to leverage the brand power of their parent organization, such as the local Salvation Army centre.

But most small charities do not have these advantages and need to stay constantly connected by building relationships with the people that count: professional advisors, community leaders and philanthropic leaders.

It's important to identify these individuals, develop a strategy to stay connected to them and work that strategy constantly. With hard work and constant attention, they can become a willing audience who is anxious to know that you are operating in a fiscally responsible and professional way with transparent and effective policies, procedures and protocols. They also can provide an outstanding sounding board of advice, objective perspective, ideas and opinions that you can access when needed.

Professional Advisors

Made up of, but not exclusive to, lawyers, accountants, financial advisors, life insurance agents, investment advisors and anyone involved directly with advising individuals on their financial and estate plans, this group is almost certainly involved at some stage of the process when a large gift is donated. They will be called upon for their expertise in transferring assets such as stocks, advice on tax matters or the establishment of endowments.

This group is both well connected and well-informed on financial matters. They are the first to examine at the bottom line. Based on what they know and believe about you, they may either encourage or dissuade a potential donor.

Community Leaders

This group is made up of government, political, community and business leaders. All of these individuals can influence the way people think about the organization. This is especially true in smaller centres. Respect for the organization and the way it operates does get around. People talk, often. When they talk about the organization, and they will, ensure that they say good things – and to the right people.

Strive to provide political figures with good news stories that they can take to the public. Show social service sector leaders the results of the financial support your organization has received. Tell financial stories to business leaders. Finally, seek out government staff that can connect your cause to appropriate government agencies. If you are a local environmental group, for example, you should probably meet with local planning department staff. Children's charities can meet with youth and child services professionals. The connections are easy to make and invaluable as a way to get the message out.

Philanthropic Leaders

Community givers are a key audience for any group. They bring with them a unique perspective because they contribute to many organizations that make a transformational difference to the community and its causes. As such, they will provide you with honest feedback about your case for giving, will tell you if your marketing messages resonate with them and others, and show you where your processes need improvement. Plus, of course, if they are impressed with you and your work, they will either give you money or lead you to it.

A small charity that raised funds for services to the elderly learned the benefits of philanthropic connections. After it had done some extensive work to revitalize its mission and its core capacity, it went out to the community to test its assumptions. The very first philanthropic leader who was approached listened intently and immediately made an emotional and practical connection with the organization's destiny proposition and its operational processes. He became the organization's largest donor, ever.

This was good fortune, but the organization learned another key lesson. Emboldened by the success of its first major philanthropic effort, it stopped connecting to other potential donors. It lost its momentum and missed further opportunities. Once the outreach begins, it cannot stop. If you build it, they will come, but you had better be prepared and keep building.

There are three simple ways to connect with these groups: personal visits, group presentations and targeted information mailings. Each of these strategies will take varying levels of time and resources to implement. However, they are cost-effective and easy to set up and execute.

Personal visits or "narrow-casting" your message

Connecting on a face-to-face basis with advisors is much like doing so with donors. It is a simple way to advance the relationship between the organization and the individual.

Create a simple presentation no more than 15 minutes long. Outside of the standard core mission items that must accompany any presentation, highlight the work done by the organization to build its capacity. Spend time to explain how the organization regulates and reports financial matters. Discuss the efforts made to increase your governance and operating standards. Finally, include numbers and facts. Every donor wants to know the intended and real outcomes (or results) of their gift. Leave time for questions. Try to be in and out in 30 minutes or less, unless the discussion is a good one and there are obvious signs of interest.

Finally, strive to get a business card, ask if you can reconnect at a later time and then ensure that this happens.

Segmented outreach or "mid-casting"

Aimed at very specific groups, such as core donors, professionals, church leaders, animal rights activists and so on, the objective is to appeal to wide number of people who can empathize with your story, tell it to others and connect you to a broader range of donors. These "touches" also raise awareness of your core mission and provide good, practical information to professionals who may be pivotal in encouraging others to give.

Reporting to the community or "broadcasting"

As long as you can do it cost-effectively and carefully, it is always a good idea to make your financial situation as widely known as possible. Never underestimate the power of being open and transparent to spread the word that you are a fiscally responsible and successful organization.

One small charity that funds student trips overseas does a three-minute monthly "talk show" on its local radio station. Recently, it used this time to highlight its financial progress over the previous three years. The story was a good one; funds raised had increased by 20% annually, costs associated with the effort had decreased and more money than ever had been made available to the cause.

Within four days of the broadcast, the organization received $8,000 in donations. ll those who gave did so because they had heard the "good news" on the radio and were impressed. This may not always happen to you. But it's a great example of the power of effective financial storytelling.

Notes about the "Case"

An essential part of the marketing plan, the Case for Support has been for many years, a key component of the organization's attempt to articulate its destiny proposition. Often times though, the case focuses too closely on the organization's immediate needs and doesn't create a sense of a larger purpose. Below are some things to think about when creating your case for support:

Ten things to ask about the Case for Support

1. Does the Case Statement articulate a vision larger than the institution itself?

2. Does the Case Statement discuss urgent need?

3. Does the Case Statement appeal to a broad cross section of the community?

4. Can the Case Statement withstand scrutiny?

5. Does the Case Statement address the future as well as the present?

6. Is the Case Statement memorable?

7. Does the Case Statement provide a rational and emotional argument?

8. Is the Case Statement and affirmation of your mission?

9. Is the Case Statement easily read and understood, give clear indication of donor giving opportunities and include an Executive Summary?

10. Is the Case Statement clear about the need and provide attainable goals?

CHAPTER 13:
CALLING IN THE CAVALRY

A common question asked by many smaller charities is, "Should we hire a consultant?"

It's a good question, because fundraising is complex and challenging, and very few are qualified to do it effectively. Organizations often feel that hiring a consultant will help them to achieve their targets much more easily than if they were left to do it on their own. But these same organizations may not truly understand what a consultant actually brings to the table. Many groups feel that the consultant's primary role is to raise the money and that they can relax their own efforts as a result. These organizations often measure the consultant's success by the amount of money they have raised.

But most consultants do not focus on direct fundraising nor do they raise money on their own. Instead, they focus on increasing the organization's capacity so that its Board, staff and volunteers are better positioned to raise the funds themselves in both the short- and long-term. The best consultants truly focus on building this long term capacity, based on the age-old notion that if "give a man a fish you may feed him for a day. Teach a man to fish and you will feed him for a lifetime." Consultants are teachers, facilitators, educators, motivators. They will lead you to the money, but you must raise it.

Consultants can be used to assist with the development of the fundraising plan. Could they also be hired to do the audit? They can identify potential targets, develop the case statement, and often assist with many of the more difficult "asks" required in a campaign. It is well known that consultants will often coordinate an entire campaign: setting up a campaign office, recruiting and training volunteers and staff, and carrying out all the day-to-day administration tasks that are required to make a campaign successful.

They can also help to hire new professionals for an organization, build a successful back room operation or develop the right messaging and branding to use in community engagement efforts. Consultants are valuable when they bring a key set of skills, experience and knowledge to an organization that does not currently possess. You need to be very clear what skills you need and how they can best be applied before you hire a consultant. For example, a consultant can provide you with real-life scenarios of what can go wrong if incorrect practices are used or research is poorly applied.

Ask the Right Questions!

Working with a consultant is only going to be effective if an organization asks itself some hard questions in advance.

1. **What do we want a consultant to accomplish?** Consultants can be used to provide strategic advice or to offer objective perspectives on a campaign plan. Because they have been involved in many campaigns and seen many situations, this advice and guidance can be invaluable in helping you avoid mistakes and to chart an effective course of action.

   Consultants can also be used for very specific tasks. For example, they may be able to help you to do a feasibility study to see if your campaign can be "sold" and if the giving climate in your target area will support it. They can set an effective target or write the marketing materials required to develop and sell your message. Sometimes, consultants are asked to assist with the approach to major donors, and, as noted, may even set up the interviews and conduct the meetings with significant prospects.

   Consultants may even take a formal title or position in the organization, such as Executive Director or Campaign Coordinator, and in this admin-istrative capacity take on the work of a staff member on a contract basis.

   The important thing is to be crystal clear about the reasons that you need a consultant. This means you should assess your own in-house capabilities and resources and find out where you have gaps that the consultant can sensibly fill. Remember too the famous saying from Stephen Covey: "Start with the end in mind." Be very specific about what you want a consultant to achieve. Otherwise, as the old Irish saying goes, "if you don't know where you are going, any road will take you there." There are literally thousands of fundraising consultants in North America, many of them exceptionally competent and leaders in the field. But you run a significant risk of not hiring the correct person for the job you need if you have not clearly defined that need in the first place.

2. **To whom will the consultant report?** This is a crucial issue, because consultants need good structures and processes in order to be able to work effectively. They need someone to report to and to be accountable for their actions. Very often it is time-consuming and difficult to manage the work of a consultant, and it is important that you have someone on board who has experience in working with paid professionals and can not only validate their decisions, but assist them appropriately. In short, you need a chain of command.

3. **What kind of personality are you looking for?** This is crucial, because fundraising history is littered with examples of organizations and consultants who just simply did not get along. You need to make sure the consultants have the personality, skill set, communication abilities and relationship strengths that will be a good fit with your volunteer board and your team as a whole.

4. **Similarly, what kind of experience will be helpful?** There is no point hiring a consultant who has spent two decades dealing with multi-million dollar projects, when you are only looking to raise $500,000. You need a consultant who has direct experience in the type of campaign you wish to run, the amount of money you are seeking, the culture and environment in which you are working and a wide range of other factors, not the least of which is successful completion of similar campaigns.

Recently at a conference held by a large fundraising association, a consultant was discussing the best way to bring together an organization's major gift and planned gift programs. The consultant began – as most speakers do – by outlining her professional experience, in this case primarily with large institutions accustomed to receiving many substantial gifts annually.

But on this particular day, the room was filled with planned giving officers from smaller organizations. One asked about the best way to make a planned giving approach to a major gift donor who gave a yearly gift of $10,000.

What happened next was an exercise of "broken telephone," as the consultant tried to convince the planned giving officer that if someone gives $10,000 per year they are an annual donor and not a major gift donor. The experience of the two professionals was so different it was as if they were speaking a different language while using the same terms and concepts.

5. **What process should we use to find a consultant?** There are many ways to approach this task. One approach is to ask other organizations that have run successful campaigns for contact names and references. Members of your own organization may know consultants who have succeeded in similar projects elsewhere. Another route to go is the request for proposal (RFP) route. This involves developing a specific proposal that outlines your needs, and will include an overview of your organization and its target, your expectations for the work to be performed, the kind of fee structure you may have to pay, the timelines for the campaign and other pertinent data.

   Requests for proposal are often used when you want to cast a wide net to find the very best consultant possible. But before you issue your own RFP, get help from someone who has experience in drafting and circulating RFPs so that you don't end up attracting a large number of applicants who don't have the appropriate experience to manage your situation.

6. **What kind of working arrangements do we need?** Again, there are many options. You can hire a consultant on a monthly or annual retainer basis to carry out a variety of very specific tasks. Consultants will often also work on the basis of several hours per week, and be recompensed accordingly. Sometimes, consultants will sign on full time for a relatively short

period (three to six months) to get a campaign up and running, and then drop back to a less rigorous schedule as the campaign progresses. Some consultants are simply hired on the basis of an hourly fee that is used whenever the organization wants advice and consultation. Be very clear about what the costs of any contractual arrangement are, and make sure, of course, that you can pay for them!

7. **Here's a footnote.** Qualified fundraising consultants will not accept payments based on the amount raised, or reward and incentive schemes based on whether or not a target is achieved. Such practices are considered unethical by major fund raising associations in North America and you should be wary of anyone who offers to be compensated on this basis.

8. **How will we measure success and evaluate performance?** Because fundraising, is such a long-term venture, it is often good to have bench-marks for performance established based on different time periods in the campaign. For example, after the first three months it may be reasonable to expect to have the campaign plan developed, the case statement written, the campaign team formed, and the target groups clearly established. You would measure and evaluate your consultant's performance on the basis of the successful accomplishment of these tasks as they relate to the time line established.

9. **Can we manage this campaign "from the inside"?** Very often, running a successful campaign is about being able to bring in some help from the outside while still effectively running the project from the inside.

In other words, you need to make sure that you can carry out the advice of the consultant, put those ideas to work, and do all the necessary tasks that are required to achieve your target.

If you do not have this "inside" capacity, you may be already setting up a consultant for failure. A good consultant is often the only as good as he or she is allowed to be. So, make sure you have the internal resources required to make hiring a consultant worthwhile in the first place.

Here are 10 tips to help you decide if you need a consultant:

1. **You have no previous experience of running campaigns.** In this case, a consultant can help you get up and running very quickly and effectively, or at the very least, can help you clarify and focus on what it is you want to achieve and how you can get it done.

2. **You lack skill sets in certain areas.** As noted, this will help you decide what kind of a consultant you require and what talents she can provide for you.

3. **You need focus and clarity.** Good consultants can often help you figure out exactly what it is you need to do and when you need to do it, something that volunteer organizations often struggle with.

4. **You need to benchmark off other campaigns.** Consultants with appropriate experience can bring the lessons they have learned from other campaigns to help you. This will avoid costly mistakes and errors as you go forward.

5. **You need to keep your feet to the fire.** Because you are actually paying for help and experiencing a financial outlay to do so, you become a lot more disciplined and determined to accomplish your task. Otherwise you will have wasted time and money that you can ill afford. Consultants with good people and communication skills can help to keep a volunteer team on track without appearing to do so – and often with very good results.

6. **You need credibility.** If you are not that well known in the marketplace and your board is not particularly high profile, a good consultant can lend you "street cred" particularly when it comes to developing "the ask" for large campaign contributions. You give yourself immediate status and reputation if the consultant you hire comes with an excellent track record and image.

7. **You need confidence.** Again, even though your cause is good and your spirit is willing, you may lack the confidence required to organize or coordinate a useful campaign. Consultants are in the business of providing confidence and this may be just what you need.

8. **You are not sure what questions to ask yourself.** A good consultant will consistently probe and challenge your assumptions about your task. For example, the question, "Who will make a good campaign leader?" will provoke discussion. It may even make you realize that your original choice for campaign chair might have been a disaster!

9. **You need organization skills.** Often the enthusiasm and passion that drives campaigns also creates organizational trouble. There may be a tendency to try and complete too many tasks at once, or to complete them in the wrong order and sequence. A worthwhile consultant will develop a very logical, orderly and structured approach to fund raising and also help you to realize that the achievement of a campaign targets is not dissimilar to the successful execution of a military campaign.

10. **You need success.** Fundraising in any climate is difficult. Competition for the dollar is fierce. Competition for good people to help you raise dollars is even fiercer. There is absolutely no guarantee of success, no matter how worthy your cause or organization. Hiring a good consultant not only helps you to bring discipline and focus to your task, it reduces the risk of failure and enables you to move forward with optimism.

Don't shoot yourself in the foot

Once you have hired a consultant, avoid shooting yourself in the foot by making these very common – and often tragic – mistakes. So, don't:

1. **Expect the consultant to validate all of your ideas and suggestions.** A good consultant is an independent business professional, with his or her own track record of success. You have hired him to give you the very best advice possible, not to tell you that all your ideas and suggestions are

good. In fundraising, the client or customer is not always right. Because it is such a specialized field, with its own very rigorous discipline, many clients make well-intentioned suggestions that are, in fact, completely wrong and counterproductive. So, empower your consultant to challenge and question anything that he or she feels it is not necessarily in your best interest, no matter how close it may be to your heart!

2. **Fail to take advice.** You are paying for the very best professional advice possible, so don't turn around as soon as it is offered and reject it out of hand. This happens far more frequently than you may imagine. Of course, there should be a balance between what the consultant recommends and what the client genuinely believes is the right thing to do. But you need to trust that the consultant will always try to give you advice that is in your best interest. There is no point in requesting this and then ignoring the advice completely. Let results be your guide. You will know very quickly if you are getting "the goods" or not. If not, end the relationship. But if so, don't challenge the advice just for the sake of challenging it.

3. **Set one consultant up against another.** Again, you would be surprised how many organizations hire a second consultant to debunk or challenge the work of the first. Not only is it grossly unfair to the consultants involved, it is unprofessional.

4. **Set unrealistic goals and expectations.** Consultants are human like everybody else; they want to please and they want to help clients succeed. Sometimes this means that they may agree to expectations that are truly unrealistic and are doomed to fail. Be careful, as noted, that you do not hire a "yes man." But also make sure that your expectations are realistic from the outset. A small university in a northern state once decided to raise $20 million in eleven months. The consultants told them it could not be done, given the very small target market and economic health of the region it served. The university fired the consultant and went ahead with the campaign anyway. To almost no one else's surprise, it failed miserably,

raising only $1.6 million in the campaign. It has been deficit financing ever since.

5. **Practice a master-servant relationship.** Your consultant should be a full partner in your fundraising process, not just a servant who will carry out your every wish. Think of the relationship as a delicate balance of power and influence. You have the power to finance the campaign and make the final decisions. The consultant has the influence that enables you to do this effectively.

   If you give the consultant the power to make decisions that ultimately should rest with you, you abandon any accountability for the project, and lose that vital personal touch that fundraising requires. On the other hand, if you do not accept the influence of the consultant and integrate it into your decision-making, you are not capitalizing on the time and talent available to you.

6. **Make the consultant the fall guy for failure.** Ultimately, it is you and your Board who are responsible for the success or failure of the campaign. This includes accountability for the quality of the consultant you hire and the decisions that you make. You may find someone who is not particularly talented, in which case you need to get rid of him as soon as possible. But if you sign on and everyone works as hard as possible for success that does not happen, don't duck that responsibility by blaming someone else. The success (and it will be success!) will always be yours. If failure should occur, the same applies.

CHAPTER 14:

RENEWING THE MATRIX —

"WASH, RINSE AND REPEAT"

"Wash, rinse and repeat." You see these directions on the back of most shampoo bottles. What works for shampoo can work for organizations. Only in this case, the phrase is: "Audit, recommend, implement, repeat." Constant re-evaluation must take place. Times and best practices change constantly.

An organizational review is important and should be done regularly. Without it, weaknesses in capacity can become evident. The organization can fall back into familiar bad habits. Advances made can be lost. Time and money can end up being wasted. Constant review and renewal should be the watchword: "Wash, rinse and repeat."

Consider the organization that underwent an operational review because of a crisis. For many years it had relied heavily on a senior administrator who provided regular reporting on all the organization's operations and finances. As long as the reports continued to arrive and could be fully explained, other senior members of staff and the Board of Directors felt comfortable with the process.

After many years of controlling the reporting in this way, the senior manager left and took with him all the idiosyncratic practices of the organization and all real knowledge of how it was run.

Having failed to implement a staff succession plan and with no true record of how all operations had been conducted, the Board found itself at a clear disadvantage. It had failed to fulfill its role as a proper watchdog for the charity, had not held itself accountable for all its actions and had relied far too heavily on one individual to keep the engine turning over.

The Board and staff now found themselves unable to understand the basic financial operations and had to commission extensive research by its newly hired administrator and a neophyte Board treasurer.

The good news was that they found no unlawful or fraudulent practices. The bad news was that they began to see a financial picture that was not as solid as they had once believed. In fact, the charity was essentially insolvent, a fact kept under wraps for years by the previous administrator and never uncovered by the Board.

It was only then that the Board decided to implement best practices immediately and to review them regularly-something that should have been happening frequently in the past.

The goal of constant re-evaluation is to increase transparency and capacity while challenging assumptions and current practices. To be done well, it needs to be part of a regular process, given as a responsibility to an individual or committee and reported and presented regularly to the Board.

The prepared organization today can become the unprepared organization of the very near future if efforts are not made to revitalize EVERY process that gives confidence to internal and external stakeholders. With this in place, gathering the support that is to needed to make the world a better place becomes a lot less difficult!

CHAPTER 15:
A FINAL THOUGHT

Being Worthy and Prepared is a journey. Leadership is the compass necessary to guide you. The ultimate goal of every charitable organization is to make the world a better place by fulfilling its destiny proposition: that may be through elimination of hunger, finding a cure for cancer or whatever the organization has set out to accomplish. How it goes about fulfilling that proposition is as unique to that organization as the people involved with it and the community it serves. The destiny proposition of the organization comes from the core values that helped to create it in the first place and that are constantly being examined and redefined by those who govern it, operate it and are served by it.

Organizations that commit to the creation and fulfillment of the Destiny Proposition are imbued with a "culture of worthiness." This recognizes that every single thing they do, from the most routine to the most breath-taking all contribute to their worthiness – or lack of it – in the eyes of their most important target group, the donor.

To have any chance to create this culture, the organization requires leadership that demands the highest level of practice, process, policy and procedure – the fundamentals of the Prepared Matrix. Without this, no organization will survive for long. Only with this culture – and with this level of preparation and attention to detail – can it truly be Worthy and Prepared.

Some years ago, Jean Edward Smith, a professor of American History and Government at the University of Toronto (a transplanted American now teaching at Ashland University in Ohio) wrote a column for Toronto's *Globe and Mail* newspaper. In it he took the time to show the distinction between management and leadership. It was Jean Smith's belief that management and leadership are often confused by those who hold the position that calls for one – namely leadership – but act as though they have the responsibility of the other – namely management. It was this confusion that caused 'leaders' of these organizations to make decisions that in the end were detrimental not only to the institutions and organizations that they "lead" but also to those that those institutions and organizations served.

To illustrate the difference, he quoted the late A. Bartlett Giamatti, who was once the commissioner of Major League Baseball and a former president of Yale University.

What Professor Giamatti said was this: "Management is the capacity to handle multiple problems, neutralize various constituencies and [in the charitable not-for-profit world that we have discussed] achieve a break-even budget. Leadership, on the other hand, is essentially a moral act, not – as in most management – an essentially protective act. It is the assertion of a vision, not simply the exercise of style: the moral courage to assert a vision of the institution [or organization] and the intellectual energy…to make that vision compelling."

We couldn't have said it better ourselves.

SO WHAT HAPPENED TO THE GOOD FOOD GROUP?

The Good Food Group that had met so enthusiastically that Saturday morning, only to find it both unwilling and unable to move forward, realized that they had three choices.

They could stay as they were now, essentially raising reasonably small amounts of money with events and bingo, doing most of the work themselves and with the help of the core staff and the Executive Director who had recognized her own inadequacies when it came to raising funds.

In doing this, they accepted that significant growth would always elude them. They would always be an operational organization, doing great work but on a very small scale and at considerable cost to themselves, both in terms of time and, ultimately, passion for the tasks at hand. Passion that would probably dwindle away the longer they pursued this option.

Or, they could make a leap of faith and undertake a much more significant task: raise more than $300,000 in two years, even though they did not have the knowledge or capacity to do this, perhaps with some help from a fundraising consultant.

This option, they soon worked out, would probably result in their demise. They would undertake a task for which they were both unworthy and unprepared and, in doing so, would probably not only fail but might also jeopardize what they had already worked so hard to build up. The good, solid fundamentals that had got them where they were, would be overlooked in favour of a much bigger campaign, and would probably suffer as a result.

Or, they could essentially clean house and start over. They would need to decide several key things:

• Did they really want to be a bigger operation with a destiny proposition quite different from the one they had now?

• If the answer to that was "yes," then were they prepared to find a new Executive Director who could lead them to that destiny and find ways to achieve it?

• Finally, were they prepared to change many of the comfortable practices and processes of today and undertake what was really required to become worthy and prepared tomorrow?

That conversation required another three Saturdays before it was resolved. Many creative and courageous conversations were held. Much soul-searching took place. Painful decisions were made. Tears were shed.

In the end, the Good Food Group realized that, as a small charity, they were no different from any other enterprise. They had to grow or they would stagnate. And because there were increasingly more seniors being forced onto the streets without sufficient food, stagnation was clearly not an option.

And so, after many months of work and diligence, a new Good Food Group emerged with a clear sense of its own future, a new and experienced fundraiser as Executive Director, a strong set of operational processes, a fundraising plan and a Board that retained only four of the original members that had first met in the funeral parlour all that time ago.

It had been hard but exhilarating, and it proved to be successful. The Good Food Group went on to raise over $1 million. It now serves 32% more seniors than it did before. Its volunteers are passionate about its work, and its reputation is second to none.

It has become Worthy and Prepared – and the future looks bright!

———————

www.ingramcontent.com/pod-product-compliance
Lightning Source LLC
Chambersburg PA
CBHW080556220326
41599CB00032B/6506